PERGAMON INTERNATIONAL LIBRARY
of Science, Technology, Engineering and Social Studies

The 1000-volume original paperback library in aid of education,
industrial training and the enjoyment of leisure

Publisher: Robert Maxwell M.C.

MODERN EDUCATIONAL GYMNASTICS

_____ **Publisher's Notice to Educators** _____

THE PERGAMON TEXTBOOK
INSPECTION COPY SERVICE

An inspection copy of any book suitable for use as a course text for under-
graduate or graduate students will gladly be sent for consideration for adoption
without obligation. Copies may be retained for a period of 30 days from receipt
and returned if not suitable. When a particular title is adopted or recommended
for adoption for class use and the recommendation results in a sale of 12 or more
copies, the inspection copy may be retained with our compliments. If after
examination the lecturer decides that the book is not suitable for adoption but
would like to retain it for his personal library, then our Educators' Discount of
10% is allowed on the invoiced price.

OTHER TITLES OF INTEREST:-

MODERN
EDUCATIONAL GYMNASTICS

BY

G. DOREEN PALLETT

Lady Mabel College of Physical Education,
Wentworth Woodhouse, Rotherham, Yorkshire

PERGAMON PRESS

OXFORD · NEW YORK · TORONTO
SYDNEY · PARIS · BRAUNSCHWEIG

Pergamon Press Offices:

U.K.   Pergamon Press Ltd., Headington Hill Hall, Oxford OX3 0BW,
                England

U.S.A.   Pergamon Press Inc., Maxwell House, Fairview Park,
                Elmsford, New York 10523, U.S.A.

CANADA   Pergamon of Canada, Ltd., 207 Queen's Quay West,
                Toronto 1, Canada

AUSTRALIA   Pergamon Press (Aust.) Pty. Ltd., 19a Boundary Street,
                Rushcutters Bay, N.S.W. 2011, Australia

FRANCE   Pergamon Press SARL, 24 rue des Ecoles,
                75240 Paris, Cedex 05, France

WEST GERMANY   Pergamon Press GMbH, D-3300 Braunschweig, Postfach 2923,
                Burgplatz 1, West Germany

First edition 1965
Reprinted 1975

Library of Congress Catalog Card No. 65-26352

Printed in Great Britain by *A. Wheaton & Co.*
ISBN 08 011495 4 (flexicover)
08 011496 2 (hard cover)

Contents

CONTENTS

Preface

THIS book has been written as a guide to all who are teaching Gymnastics based on Rudolf Laban's analysis of movement. It is the result of many years study and teaching of children and students. Perhaps I have been lucky as originally I was trained and felt secure in the Ling Swedish Gymnastics, passed through the stage of change and doubt and have come to an even greater security in the knowledge that Modern Educational Gymnastics has much more to offer educationally.

There was good in the "old" — a discipline, a set standard, demanding perseverance, grit and determination — but little consideration for individual ways of moving and so a limited movement vocabulary, in which one either excelled or failed. Gymnastics today provides for and gives every individual an opportunity to achieve ; the possibilities in movement are endless and not only is physical prowess of importance, but also ideas. It is the girl as a person who is of primary importance, her endeavour and attainment.

Teaching has become much more difficult as every girl has to be assessed on her own merit, but it is far more rewarding to the teacher and beneficial to the girls. It is the weak teacher who will set the girls to work and leave them — they will soon get bored — and the teacher may try to justify to herself that it is wrong to tell them what to do : but the good teacher will guide and lead the girls into discovering ways of moving and achieving skill. There must be skill and I do urge teachers to set and demand a standard just ahead of what each girl is giving, showing the class by demonstration what is considered "good" and then urging them to get even better — it is this that brings satisfaction. I feel this is essential, and unfortunately is lacking in some of the teaching today.

There are many ways of presenting the work and every teacher must find her own. The basic principles of movement are the same and these I have tried to explain and apply to gymnastic movement throughout the book. In teaching gymnastics it is only through hard work and steady progression that true satisfaction is gained.

Without the children and students I have taught, all who have taught me and particularly the help and training I had at the Art of Movement Studio, this book would not have been possible — to them all I offer my thanks and in particular to my colleague Joan Tomlinson who so patiently read the script in its early stages, and also to Mr. S. Chadwick for taking the photographs.

G. D. PALLETT

CHAPTER I

Introduction

A HUMAN being has a body, concerned with practical actions: a mind, concerned with thinking : and feeling or emotion, concerned with expression. It is impossible to separate one from the others, though in certain situations one aspect may be more involved. The creative artist, whatever his medium, whether it be stone, wood, words, paint, sound or movement calls primarily upon the feeling or expressive side of his make up, though the other aspects of his person are of necessity used in order to achieve fulfilment. The intellectual mainly uses his brain and thinking powers to solve his problems, his body and expressive abilities taking minor parts. In a practical action there is an object to be achieved involving skilful use of the body, thus the task is thought out and the body put into action to achieve the end. During the action the person will undoubtedly have certain feelings towards it and gain satisfaction from achievement, but it is primarily the skilful use of his body in co-operation with his mind, that has enabled him to fulfil the task.

Gymnastics comes into this last practical category, the aim and object being to gain mastery over the body in many and varied situations. Thought will be needed to solve problems and sensations will be experienced during and as a result of action, but the latter should never mask the practical, objective attitude of the gymnast. Expressive movement would be out of place, unprofitable and possibly dangerous. Nevertheless, gymnastics should be vital, and to be so every part of the person, body, mind and feeling, must be alive and sensitive, taking its rightful place.

1

There is a growing tendency in people only to move the arms and legs and rarely the torso, thus there is an isolation of movement which is unnatural. Perhaps this is the result of our modern civilisation, for we live in a mechanical age of press-buttons and one of watching instead of participating ourselves. So much is done by machinery working at the touch of a switch, taking the place of full body action which was necessary in the past : the mechanical drill of the road-mender instead of the swing of the pick : the combine harvester instead of the use of the scythe and pitch-fork : the electric cleaner and polisher, buses to convey children to and from school, television, cinemas and football matches to watch for amusement. All these devices and amusements give no opportunity to fulfil the natural inborn tendency to move and unless it is nurtured in the young people many may lose the urge to move and become relatively illiterate in movement, or those whose instinct is strong sometimes find challenges to their physical prowess in daring expeditions outside the law.

It is a responsibility of educationists to see that young people are given opportunity to develop as people. Movement is fundamental and involves the whole being — in fact without it a person is dead — so every chance should be given to establish good movement with the joy and satisfaction it gives in as many ways as possible in order to compensate, in some measure, for the trends of the present day, and before the natural joy of moving is completely lost.

It is still within our nature to respond to challenges which require physical skill and mental alertness, and through this, confidence is gained leading to satisfaction, self-respect and poise. Whatever the final interests and inclinations of the individual, the work in gymnastics can be a sound training and full opportunity should be taken of the facilities in the school.

To a certain extent movement is instinctive, inborn in us in order to obtain food and protect ourselves from danger. Originally it was developed to a high degree and of necessity had to be skilled in order to survive, with only the survival of the fittest and most versatile ; but those days are long past and now variety of movement and skill need to be developed and maintained in other ways. Movement is the result of nerve and muscle co-ordination, the unconscious instinctive actions of self-preservation originating in the reflex centres of the brain ; but the conscious voluntary actions involve the higher thought centres and with every new action a new neuro-muscular pathway has to be made. The more often the action is repeated the more this pathway is used and the more skilled the movement becomes. Therefore it is necessary to establish as many neuro-muscular pathways as possible to give a wide movement vocabulary and necessary to repeat the actions to achieve skill.

Every part of every gymnastic lesson should have purpose — not just a mere occupying of the class, or a time to "let off steam". It is excellent that the girls have energy and this should be used profitably ; if apparently they have none, they may need stimulating to produce it. The lesson should be vital, active and challenging, involving the whole person though the stress, due to the nature of gymnastics, will be on the mental and physical sides. Opportunity should be given to move the whole body with varying Effort rhythms in the Space, using familiar ways to give confidence and satisfaction, exploring the less familiar and responding to the challenges of the unknown. In this way there should be an increase in movement skill with economy of effort : an easy flow of logical movement with its rhythmic build up, climax and recovery : an increase in vocabulary and the ability to respond to new situations showing initiative, determination and perseverance.

As the understanding of movement grows the girls realise that not everyone moves in the same way and every task is not similarly carried out : as a result of this, independence and the ability to make decisions in the selection of movement best for the individual in the varied situations, is developed. With the varied use of apparatus as obstacles combined with the tasks set, the girls' movement understanding is applied and judgements made accordingly, thus helping them to gain in confidence in their own ability. Working with other people leads to co-operation and sensitivity to others, making them more tolerant and willing to help, taking responsibility and becoming more reliable as people — all this, and much more, can be achieved in gymnastics, contributing to the whole of the educational programme of the school.

The material of movement has been set down in the following chapters, and that of necessity has been isolated into aspects to do with the Body, the Effort content and the use of Space, but none can exist without the others. Of necessity there is a tendency to isolate; analysis is essential and the need to *stress* an aspect, but it must, when teaching, be *supported* by the rest. In the same way movement of the body cannot have purpose without that vital non-physical part of the human being. It must be remembered that it is *living people who are being taught* and not just physical activity. It is up to the teacher to set the atmosphere for full participation by each member of her class and to be aware of each individual, for every one is different — it is this which makes teaching worthwhile.

CHAPTER II

Weight Transference

THIS is a most important part of movement as it is involved in every action which is not a gesture.

A **gesture** is a movement of any part of the body which does not involve a transference of weight, whether it be of the arms or legs, which are the most usual, or of the head and spine. Gestures may lead to a transference of weight; in fact use is made of them in producing momentum or when leading a movement with a definite part of the body.

There seem to be three main ways in which the body is used when the weight is moved from one part to another, but in all of them there needs to be an understanding of *where the weight of the body is falling*, which leads to control and awareness of the action; whether it be of a more fluent off-balance nature or one of a more stable on-balance nature which can be stopped.

First of all a few words about where the body weight falls in relationship to its base or point of support. If the child is moving in an **on-balanced** way the body weight or centre of gravity falls *inside* the base. If moving in an **off-balanced** way the centre of gravity falls *outside* the base or point of support.

An **on-balanced** movement, the weight being always over the base, is one which may be either on the spot or travelling. It will be of a stable nature and can be stopped at will and the larger the base the easier it will be to perform the action. An example of moving on the spot might be that of curling and stretching whilst changing the base from both feet to one foot, to one foot and one knee, to one knee alone. Here one can feel that although the whole movement is stable there is a more difficult weight adjustment when the base is small.

It is also possible to move in this stable on-balanced way from one part of the body to another and travel ; walking is the obvious example, but in the gymnasium other parts of the body may be brought into action, the base or parts of the body continually changing, but the body weight being kept within the base.

In an **off-balanced** movement the centre of gravity falls outside the supporting base and leads to flying and falling actions. This sometimes happens at unexpected moments, as in vaulting, and it is said "the children lack control" ; if they have not experienced the feeling they may panic and hurt themselves, but if they have and are able to adjust the weight of their bodies in such a situation to that of on-balance there is little fear of them hurting themselves. Apart from the safety point of view, this off-balance movement experience is widening their movement vocabulary and is one of the joys of gymnastics as their ability grows and they know how far and for how long they are able to fly and fall. This interplay of on- and off-balanced movement should be introduced in simple ways ; at first on the floor even with mats, making the class aware of this moving of the body weight outside the base causing off-balance — such ways as starting on the knees and leaning slowly over in any direction : up to a certain point in the leaning the movement can be arrested, but as soon as the centre of gravity falls outside the base (made by the knees) the body falls — it is at this moment that the body becomes off-balance. At first, in this case, it is usually the arms which come into action providing a base with the knees, through which the centre of gravity falls, and so the body becomes again on-balance and stable ; but later with skilled weight transference stability may be achieved without the arms. Similarly other parts of the body may be used as bases to start from and others will come into action to prevent the falling body from crashing to the ground.

The above was an example of a falling movement, but it is also possible to fly, as mentioned previously ; in which case the body is propelled off-balance usually in an obliquely upward direction by either the legs or arms. If it is the legs it is possible for the original base to catch up with the flying body and again be ready to receive it as it falls downwards, when again equilibrium is achieved. The arms may also receive the weight of the flying body when using such apparatus as ropes or bars, or the arms in conjunction with other parts of the body, if flying upwards onto more stable apparatus such as a box. Besides the legs the arms are the only other parts able to lift the body into the air, in which case it is usual to land on the feet.

In many actions there are moments of both on- and off-balance and the children should be aware of and able to use both efficiently and at will. For example, in standing on the hands a girl may start with her weight balanced between feet and hands, and until the weight falls within the smaller base provided by her hands (after the push off from the feet) the movement will be off-balance and the legs will return to the ground ; when the weight is over the hands she will be on-balance ; if the legs and hips go beyond this narrow margin of stability the body is again off-balance and the legs again fall to the ground resulting in what is often referred to as the "crab position".

Voluntarily to be able to adjust the body weight in order to *move* in either an on-balanced or an off-balanced way needs much training and experience, and shows control over the adjustment of the body weight.

WAYS OF TRANSFERRING THE BODY WEIGHT

(1) USING ADJACENT PARTS OF THE BODY

Here the weight of the body is moved gradually along the body using each part consecutively — there should be no gaps in between the parts of the body taking the weight.

(a) This can be achieved by *using parts naturally (anatomically) next to each other* as in rolling forwards or backwards where each part of the spine takes the weight in turn ; a stiff area in the spine can be observed at once, for it can be seen where the vertebrae do not touch the ground consecutively. Similarly, in rolling sideways stretched out, the back, sides and front of the body take the weight, moving consecutively from one to the other. It is only the trunk that can be used in the above way and therefore the movement possibilities soon come to an end, being limited to a rocking action, particularly in the forward and backward directions, re-sulting in a repetition of the same action.

(b) To overcome this limitation it is possible to *make parts of the body*, which anatomically are not adjacent, *become so, by putting them down close to the original part* so making the movement pass directly from one part of the body to the next without any gap in between. This can be illustrated by curling up and rolling in all directions where the weight might pass from the seat along the spine to the shoulders (using adjacent parts anatomically) and then to the knees which are placed touching the shoulders (adjacent but not anatomically) to the lower leg and onto the side of the seat placed close to the legs and so on.

In all weight transference there has to be a continual adjust-ment of the body weight ; there are moments when the gymnast has to hold it back or alternatively to urge it forwards to ensure a smooth action. This is very much a matter of *how* one moves and is concerned with the Effort content of move-ment (see chapter on Effort).

In weight transference it is the **Weight Factor** that is primarily involved. In this we are dealing with the tension in the muscles ; whether it is strong, less strong or of a weak tension : there is a continual interplay and smooth transition from one degree of tension to another. This degree of tension is closely linked with where the body weight falls in relation to the point of support. The following two examples will illustrate this point :

(1) Starting on the back, stretched out and rolling sideways — the body is stable, resting on the whole of the back which is a large base ; a strong contraction of muscle is required to move the body weight onto the side ; while the body weight is moving over the side, the muscle work is easier and the muscle tension weaker, but as the movement continues and the body weight begins to fall outside this base the muscle work again has to increase and the muscle tension is stronger, this time to resist gravity to ensure the body meeting the ground gently and smoothly.

(2) Starting curled up sitting on the floor rolling backwards — the body weight is stable and falling directly through the base, in this case the seat. A weak tension will start the body moving backwards but a strong tension of muscle is required to lift the hips over the shoulders and as the body weight passes over the shoulders a weaker tension is needed, but as soon as the body weight begins to fall outside the base (shoulders) a stronger tension is again needed, just sufficient to resist the pull of gravity in order to lower the knees gently to the ground.

Thus there are **definite moments of** stronger and weaker tensions essential to **smooth** weight transference from one part of the body to another in direct relationship to the main points of support during the action ; whilst the body is moving over the point of support the tension is weaker, and when moving towards it, very strong, and moving away from it, strong enough to resist gravity.

When teaching, *awareness of both the body and the Effort content must be considered together* and experience given in many varied situations. Knowing just how much tension is required is entirely an individual thing and only comes from much practice and an understanding of what is involved. There should be no bruising and the body should travel over the floor gently and smoothly. At first the movement could be taken slowly and done with care with conscious awareness of what is happening, but as the class progresses variations of speed should be encouraged and in many cases this will make the actions easier, as the momentum gained will help the strong muscle work involved. For example, in such an action as rolling forwards and onto the feet — taken at a medium speed some children may not be able to transfer their weight onto the feet after the roll ; but if the speed is increased towards the end of the roll they should be able to achieve it ; thus an increase of speed combines with a strong tension to achieve a skilful action.

Rolling, or using adjacent parts of the body, can be done in all directions and can be combined with other aspects of movement such as bending and stretching, twisting, symmetrical and asymmetrical movement and at different speeds until full control is obtained. Besides widening movement vocabulary and ability to manage one's body, this aspect is most essential from a safety point of view and should be taught carefully and thoroughly.

Some suggestions for activities where the use of adjacent parts are involved

It is assumed that some real teaching of what is involved will have been given, though some of the simpler suggestions may be used concurrently. The teacher, knowing what movement experience she wishes to give to the class, will be able to invent many other situations. The following might be used as Introductory or Class Activities, thus putting into practice what the girls understand, increasing familiarity and ability, and giving the teacher opportunity to observe and help the individual.

Mats might be used for rolling on in all directions, or for rolling round the edge without swivelling round, but moving continuously forward, sideways and backwards : this might be done in two's, both rolling at once but avoiding each other. These ideas may be developed through a change of speed and by changing from curled to stretched rolling.

Moving freely between mats in any direction and as they come to a mat go into a roll, therefore the roll may be forwards, sideways or backwards. Again, variation in speeds will increase the skill of performance. Height also will increase the difficulty, and forms may be used in conjunction with the mats where it is necessary to get over the form by jumping or using the hands and on meeting the ground rolling and recovering.

Off-balance movement should also be experienced in such a way as balancing in stillness on a part of the body and toppling over into a roll and recovering ; this may be progressed from the knees up to the hands as starting off points. Gradually height can be increased by using the forms from which to fall and recover through rolling. So far the overbalancing has been quite voluntary and therefore completely prepared for, but something of the unexpected may be introduced in such game-like activities as meeting an opponent on a narrow form or bar and trying to overbalance her ; here the moment and direction of off-balance is not known and the girls have to adapt to the unexpected.

These are a few suggestions, starting at floor level progressing through a combination of locomotion, height, narrowness and concentration on something other than the main aspect of movement concerned ; thus the teacher will be able to observe the standard of skill the class has achieved. By now the girls should be able to meet the ground from a low level, being able to transfer their weight easily and smoothly in any direction from and onto a great variety of parts of the body and should be safe even if they fall accidentally.

The low large apparatus could now be used, such as bars, box or double forms, where the task set might be "Get on and come off with hands or feet meeting the ground followed by a roll". Getting on to the apparatus using different parts of the body should be encouraged as it leads to coming off in different ways, but since the stress and primary training at this moment is in coming off, the getting on is of secondary importance and can be stressed in later lessons. The height of the apparatus can gradually be increased as the ability of the class increases.

Besides transferring the weight using adjacent parts of the body in the coming off from the apparatus, it is possible to do so whilst on the apparatus, but here length is needed and the task might be "Get on, roll along the apparatus and get off". Any apparatus is suitable which has length and sufficient width. The rolling may be curled up or stretched out and could be in any direction. The class are able to come off safely and in a variety of ways so this will now take second place and the going along may be coached primarily ; thus by stressing different parts of the vault the whole is gradually improved.

CHAPTER III

Weight Transference

(2) USING NON-ADJACENT PARTS OF THE BODY

IN THIS section is included the transference of weight from one part of the body to another, using parts which are not adjacent to each other, thus missing out a part or parts in between. Some examples are such actions as walking, where the weight is moved from one foot to the other; walking on hands and feet; moving from one foot or both feet to one or both hands; moving from the shoulders to the feet. One steps, as it were, from one part of the body to another.

Here the body weight has to be *moved further* than when rolling since neighbouring parts of the body have been omitted, so that the Effort content (see chapter on Effort), especially the Weight Factor, will be greater. Following on from the above will be the fact that the further away the receiving part of the body is from the point of "take-off", the greater the strength needed to achieve the action : for example in the task of "Moving from feet to hands" the closer the hands can be put to the feet, the easier it will be to lift the body weight from the feet to the hands; the further away the hands, the greater the distance the body weight has to be moved and therefore the greater the strength required.

In order to move the body weight with the least effort, it is necessary to *start with it over the base*, since this part of the body has to propel it in the direction required and transfer it through the air to fall directly *over the receiving base*. This adjustment of the body weight is directly concerned with how much tension is required in the muscles at various moments in the action. Taking the same action of "moving from feet to hands", a strong tension is needed to lift the hips upwards and forwards over the hands, but a weaker tension is required whilst over the hands, just sufficient to resist the pull of gravity which falls through the base (hands). Skill is only attained after much considered practice in judging just the amount of strength needed and the transitions from stronger to weaker tensions.

There are other factors too affecting this weight transference such as the speed of moving — when considering the use of adjacent parts of the body we saw that an increase of speed at certain moments made it possible to lessen the degree of tension in order to achieve the action more easily ; similarly in this case ; therefore practice in using variation of speed in conjunction with variation of tension leads to greater skill. Another factor is the use of only one limb to push off from or land onto, rather than two, requiring greater tension in that one limb, as it has to work twice as hard.

The legs are much stronger than the arms, therefore it is easier to push off from or land onto the lower rather than the upper limbs. However, the hips being the heaviest part of the body greater strength is needed to move them than any other part of the body.

Opportunity should be given to explore and experiment in the use of as great a variety of combinations of parts of the body as possible, with an awareness of what part is being moved from and what part is being moved onto, together with an awareness of the varying tensions and speeds needed to move the body weight economically and efficiently.

Some suggestions of activities where non-adjacent parts
  of the body are used

The most usual parts of the body used are the hands and feet, but other parts may be used in conjunction with the above.

Progression of activities should be gradual starting at floor level either on the floor or with mats leading onto the use of forms, low apparatus and finally higher apparatus. For example, moving from the feet (it can be either one or both feet) onto the hands and back to the feet (either one or both). These can be done with the body either curled or stretched or with a twist and the directions forwards, backwards and sideways used. Among the above activities may be recognised activities known as "walking on all fours", "bunny jumps", "handstands" and "cartwheels" as well as many other possible variations. With the understanding of the movement possibilities involved the teacher can observe the variations given by the girls and can select from them and let the whole class try them ; or lead them by movement suggestions to a more complete repertoire, thus increasing the children's "vocabulary". Isolated actions of weight transference are a starting-off point, but very soon they should be linked together to make a continuous sequence of movement involving a variety of parts of the body as, for example, from the feet onto hands onto one foot to the seat onto one knee to the shoulders to the feet and so on.

Small apparatus, such as a hoop, may be used when working with a partner, one holding the hoop either vertically or horizontally and the other one either going through or in and out of the hoop respectively, using non-adjacent parts of the body.

There are many possibilities when travelling along the length of a form when the body weight is taken on the hands and feet alternately. The form itself provides many variations, for the hands may be placed both on the form ; both on the floor with one on either side of the form ; both on the floor with both on the same side of the form ; or one on the form and one on the floor. Similarly, the above will also apply to where the feet are placed in relationship to the form. Thus already there are many variations and combinations possible which lead to a greater awareness and co-ordination of the body. The weight always goes from the feet to the hands alternately but from the actual way of moving the "take-off" may be from one or both feet, the weight received by one or both hands, the body curled or stretched or twisted, and the girl may travel along the form forwards, backwards, sideways or in a combination of these ways. The action may be taken slowly or quickly and with just enough tension to clear the form if going over from side to side or with strong tension lifting the hips high into the air above the form. Various combinations of the Effort content lead to a rhythmic sequence of movement involving contrasts and interplay of the Time and Weight Factors (see chapter on Effort). In the same way other parts of the body may be used ; some are profitable, others less so ; opportunity should be given to discover this and help given, if necessary, to select or reject.

If using low bars, the children may go over, as there is no wide surface on which they can land. Therefore they must have the confidence to go right over, taking their body weight on their arms and be able to move the body weight from the point of take-off (feet) to the point of landing (feet) on the other side of the bar. As the girls become more skilled the hips will pass over the bar above their arms which will be taking their weight, and a true transference of weight from feet to hands to feet will be achieved. Children often find travelling along the bar from side to side continuously more difficult than a single weight transference over. Also they may find going over the bar more difficult than the form, for even at its lowest it is usually higher than a single form, though the lesser width of the bar should be easier to negotiate.

The bars may be used at about hip height, where the children can transfer their weight from the floor to the bars using various parts of the body in turn. For example they can start from the feet on the floor to the seat on the bar, then turn onto their "middles" on the bar, then onto their hands on the floor and so onto their feet on the floor. It is possible to support the body weight by hanging from the bar by the knees or elbows and gripping with the feet in various ways, thus giving scope for agility in managing the body weight.

Travelling along the apparatus transferring the body weight from one part to another involves a careful adjustment of weight and can be made more skilled by the apparatus used, thus giving scope for movement often referred to as **balancing**. Progression can be made by using wide apparatus at first and then narrower ; by increasing the height and, to give even more scope for skill, by using movable apparatus, such as a turned form placed at right angles over another piece of apparatus, rather like a see-saw, and as the girl travels along and up the apparatus it tips with her weight and she has to adjust to the moving apparatus and to the change from ascending to descending the form. Obstacles may be used which have to be negotiated which may involve a stepping over or getting through, such as a hoop held horizontally or vertically midway along the apparatus ; working with a partner in conjunction with the progression along the apparatus, such as passing each other mid-way and then continuing, here being independent except at the moment of passing. It is also possible to work *together* relying on each other the whole time for the careful adjustment of each other's weight, either progressing together along the apparatus or, in the case of movable apparatus, starting at opposite ends.

In all cases, the wider the base on the apparatus the easier it is, so there will be a progression by aiming to use smaller areas of the body, for example travelling along a form or bar using the feet and hands alternately is easier than using only the feet. The nearer the body is to the apparatus the easier it will be, the centre of gravity being lower, the further away it is taken the higher the centre of gravity and therefore the more difficult, for example creeping along a bar is easier than walking along on tip-toe.

The weight may be suspended from the arms in turn, rather than supported as in previous examples, **travelling** along a high bar from hand to hand or from hands to parts of the legs : the principle of moving the body weight from one to the other is the same. If using only the hands, before actual travelling along the bar is attempted, the ability to move the weight of the suspended body from one hand to the other on the spot, should be achieved. This is done by a strong bending then a releasing of the tension of the elbows alternately, which will make the body swing ; this momentum produced will make the muscle work easier. If, when facing the bar, an overgrasp is taken, the swing will be from side to side. If facing the upright, the swing will be forwards and backwards. It should be noted here that it is the strength of the arms and muscles of the shoulder girdle which should initiate this swing and not the lower part of the body. After a little practice this stage will be achieved with ease and it will be possible to lift each hand in turn off the bar, thus completely transferring the weight from one hand to the other. So far the stress of the pull has been equal in both directions, but now if it is accented in one direction, an uneven swing results enabling a step to be taken along the bar with the free hand. When this is achieved with ease, the hands may be turned and the grip on the bar changed as the step is taken, and the girl is able to change from travelling sideways to forwards to backwards at will.

Ropes may also be used when the arms and legs can take the weight alternately in order to **climb** the rope. The arms support the weight whilst the legs are bent and a firm grip taken on the rope with the feet and often the knees as well ; these then take the weight and strongly stretch whilst the hands move up the rope. This alternation continues until the height required up the rope is achieved. To come down the movement is made in reverse, the legs taking the weight whilst the hands move down the rope, then the arms whilst the legs move down. Sliding down by loosening the grip with hands and legs is dangerous, as the rope causes friction and nasty burns may result, therefore coming down the rope should be taught *before* the girls are allowed to go to the top of the rope. In the past much time was spent teaching a definite style of grip in climbing ; it was a good one for some, but not all girls found it satisfactory, so it is much better to teach the fundamentals, then let each girl find out the best way for her as an individual.

When the large portable apparatus is used at a suitable height for the class, the teacher needs to remember that the girls have to get on and off the apparatus, and these two parts of the vault need concentrating on before what happens in between. In previous examples no distinction or stress has been made, but now due to the nature of the apparatus the teacher needs to be more aware of them. She may find it necessary to stress either or both in turn.

In getting onto apparatus such as double forms, box or horse, the "take-off" is usually off the feet or hands, but various parts of the body may come to rest on the apparatus. Thus the body weight is changed from one part of the body to a non-adjacent part. This can be done either with or without the use of the hands, though normally the hands may be allowed to assist in the weight transference from the feet to such parts as "middles", seats, hip, knee(s), foot or feet. At first the girls can get off in any way, as they are concentrating on getting onto the apparatus. The possibilities of getting onto the apparatus with various parts of the body contacting it ; using various areas of the apparatus ; and meeting it facing in various directions and taking off from both hands and feet should be explored. An attitude of readiness and concentration should be encouraged in order to attack the problem in hand, using a suitable approach to the apparatus in direction, length, speed and strength, with a crescendo up to the moment of "take-off" from the floor if from the feet, so that the body "arrives" on the apparatus rather than crawls onto it.

There are several ways of **getting off the apparatus,** but there are only two main parts of the body which initially meet the ground first, taking the weight, namely the feet and the hands, though the weight may be transferred onto other parts after the first meeting. *If the landing is on the feet* the weight

could have been on any part of the body on the apparatus
such as the hands, the shoulders, the seat or even the feet ;
and it is possible for both feet to take the weight, or one foot
after the other, depending on the height of the apparatus and
the adjustment of the body weight. If the weight is falling
directly downwards it will probably be on both feet, the body
being on-balance and the centre of gravity falling well within
the base. If the weight is not falling directly over the feet it
may be taken by each foot in turn or transferred to some other
part such as the hands, only gradually becoming on-balance.

If it is the hands which meet the ground first, the fact that
the girls have previously had to get off the apparatus quite
freely, will have given them some chance to explore the possibilities as well as to use the familiar rolling ways, in which
adjacents parts of the body come into action, but now has
come the moment to bring further possibilities to their consciousness and perhaps widen their experience. If the task
set is "To get onto the apparatus with any part of the body,
but to come off onto the hands", this narrows down the ways
of getting off and so leads them to investigate further and
explore more deeply into the ways of getting off.

They will have found it possible to get onto the apparatus
with practically any part of the body, but now they will have
to adjust to the possible ways of coming off onto their hands,
which calls for a certain selection of what part to "arrive"
with, on the apparatus. From any height of apparatus it should
be possible to leave from such a part as "middles", the weight
going onto the arms, the hands placed firmly on the floor near
to the apparatus to receive the body weight, the hips lifted
upwards over the hands, either bent or stretched, and then
to descend onto the feet. If the girl has her seat on the
apparatus, the hands may be placed squarely on the floor
after bending backwards and then the legs swing over. Time
should be given to explore further possibilities of taking the
weight on the arms prior to the feet meeting the ground. It is
possible to leave the apparatus from various parts of the body,

even the knees if it is low, but the higher it gets the more difficult the task becomes and very gradual training of the taking of the now-falling body weight onto the arms is necessary. In all cases the arms need to be directly under the body weight so that they are in the best position to carry it, even though it may only be momentarily ; this adjustment of the body weight over the support and the placing of the hands in the right place need care.

Transference of weight whilst on the apparatus can be a further progression from the task of "Get on and off the apparatus" which might result in "Get on, go along and get off the apparatus". Previous examples under Balancing and Travelling may also be included at this point as they involve a weight transference along apparatus. Care must be taken in the choice of apparatus to give length and so the opportunity to fulfil the task. Here there will be an arrival on the apparatus on one part of the body and a transference of weight onto at least one other part before leaving. This can lead to a lot of scrambling about, rather pointlessly, and guidance is needed in making a sequence of the whole, but it does give scope for a wider choice of parts of the body used, and requires greater skill in adjusting the weight. On the other hand time must be given to explore the possibilities of what parts of the body are suitable to take weight on the apparatus. It is up to the teacher and her class to have an understanding whether the hands count in this or not — so often it is necessary and natural for the hands to assist that perhaps their use should be allowed in addition to other parts.

When going along it is essential to use the length of the apparatus whether approached lengthways or sideways ; for example, with the pommels on the horse there are at once three areas to be used — similarly with the long surface of the box, and the coming off from the apparatus can be from either the sides or the ends.

The teacher must decide whether she is willing to accept the use of adjacent parts of the body (rolls) in conjunction with the non-adjacent parts or whether she is keeping strictly to the use of non-adjacent parts. There is a time for both — but the important thing is that the girls must know what is required of them and that they fulfil the task set with understanding.

CHAPTER IV

Weight Transference

(3) USING NON-ADJACENT PARTS OF THE BODY
WHERE FLIGHT IS INVOLVED

HERE the body is propelled into the air, pushing off one part
and then coming down either onto the same or some other
part of the body. The whole body can be seen momentarily
flying through the air.

The most obvious parts of the body to take off from and
land onto are the legs, where it is possible to push off one
foot and land on the same foot ; to push off one foot and land
on the other foot ; to push off one foot and land on both feet ;
to push off both feet and land on one foot and finally to push
off both feet and land on both feet. These are often referred
to as *the five basic jumps*. They may be used in any combination
or separately, forming sequences of rhythmic jumps without
apparatus or in conjunction with small apparatus such as
hoops, canes, mats, forms or spring-boards. Variety and skill
may be achieved by development through the use of different
directions, speeds and tensions.

In every case the body weight should be over the point of
take-off whether it be one or both feet, so that the strength
of the legs can lift the body into the air. Even greater strength
is needed in this action, as not only has the weight to be transferred, but also the body propelled unsupported through the
air. Similarly, greater strength is needed at the moment of
contact with the ground in order to receive the falling body
and a quicker but smooth release of tension to prevent jarring.
This can be seen and experienced when comparing stepping
off a form with that of jumping off a form.

Flight can be directed upwards or combined with a backwards, forwards or sideways direction as seen in a leap, with the stress either on height or distance. Perhaps the mean of the two gives the most opportunity for true flight. To attain this, more is involved than the take-off and the landing ; the passage through the air is important. To get true flight the sensation of being airborne is necessary. This is only achieved through the subtle transition from the stronger to weaker tensions. Strong tension is needed to get the body into the air and whilst it is there a releasing of that tension is required to make the body feel light and suspended and to experience the sensation of being airborne. To give time for this to be achieved the body needs to stay in the air as long as possible and therefore height will help ; but also one aims to delay the effect of the downward force of gravity by moving the top half of the body slightly backwards, or opposite to the line of flight, so delaying its inevitable fall. As the body falls to the ground a stronger tension is needed, sufficient to "catch" and so slow down the falling body gradually, but quickly released and followed by the stronger tension needed to bounce away from the floor again.

In the above example the weight has been transferred from the feet to the feet, but it is also possible to receive the weight on the arms resulting in variations of what are often referred to as "catsprings" or "dives", the arms receiving the initial weight which is quickly and smoothly transferred either to the shoulders and spine, resulting in a "roll", or back onto the feet.

Another part of the body that it is possible to push off from is the arms. The body weight must be over them and supported by them, therefore it is far more advanced than the above as the most inexperienced child can jump to a certain extent. When the girls are able to get their weight over their arms they can try pushing off them — "Jump off your arms" and landing on the feet. The arms must be strong enough to bear their weight, with the ability to adjust their weight over their arms, then they need that slight give or bend in the elbows to allow for the strong extension necessary to propel the body into the air. The stronger and quicker it is the better the result. Compare the bending of the knees before the strong stretch which lifts the body off the ground in jumping. Though the arms and legs are the most used parts of the body, other parts such as knees and shoulders together with the arms can lift the body into the air. Exploration, followed by practice to gain skill, should be taken first at floor level and progressed gradually with the use of apparatus increasing height and distance.

Some suggestions of possible activities involving flight

As previously mentioned any type of jump may be attempted without using apparatus or using small apparatus, going into, through, over or on and off. Since flight is the primary aim there should be one *main* jump, the others being only preparatory to the main action. Mats or mattresses may be used where it is possible to push off the feet from the floor and fly through the air to land on the hands. The direction of flight is forwards along the apparatus, the hands reaching forwards as far as possible and meeting the ground first, followed by the body in a direct pathway and so onto the shoulders into a "roll", or the body may be swung sideways or over the top of the arms when the feet will meet the ground after the hands. These agilities may be progressed by using a travelling "take-off" when it is also possible to push off one foot as well as both feet.

If working with a partner one of the pair can be "*something to push off from*" whilst the other jumps as high as possible, followed by a push off from her stable partner, thus getting herself higher into the air because of the double push. It is possible for *the supporting partner (No. 1) to be the most active*, "throwing" her partner into the air. One of many possibilities is if No. 1 lies on her back with legs half bent up to the ceiling, and No. 2 lies with her "middle" or seat on her partner's feet, as a starting position ; then No. 1 slightly bends her knees and strongly and quickly extends them tossing her partner into the air, to land some distance away. Opportunity should be given to explore other possible and suitable situations. Again if working in two's, they *both may be active*. No. 1 may push off in some way and then No. 2 pushes her further at the peak of her flight getting her that much higher, then allowing her (No. 1) to fall to the floor ; thus for a time she is unsupported and flies through the air. In this, timing and co-operation are essential. This may be done working in three's where the opportunity for greater flight is possible, but three minds working together is even more difficult than two. Care must be taken to release the one flying soon enough, especially her arms and legs, so that she is able to meet the ground safely.

The girls will have now experienced flight on the floor and the next consideration will be that of apparatus which involves some distance above floor level, however low the apparatus. It is possible to fly onto, fly off, fly along or over apparatus.

Some suggestions of **flying onto apparatus**

Forms may be used which will have been jumped onto and over before, but now is the time to stress the length of time spent *in the air* and the feeling of suspension before coming to the ground. Besides jumping onto the forms with the feet, it is possible to jump from the feet and land on the hands ; this may be done when using the forms lengthways or width-ways. A low box may be used ; taking off the floor from the feet and flying onto the box arriving with either the feet, the hands, or the hands and shoulders into a roll. The width and padded top of the box makes it possible to do the latter with safety.

Experience in a more upward direction of flight will be encouraged by raising the height of the apparatus gradually, the aim always being to fly through the air and land down onto the apparatus rather than to struggle up to it. Experience in a more forward direction of flight can be encouraged by moving the point of take off gradually further away from the apparatus.

Ropes or bars of hanging height, may be used to spring onto from the feet. It is essential to get the feeling of the push-off, then the flight, followed by the pull on the arms, the height of the apparatus and distance between the take-off and the apparatus should be increased gradually and progress made to a moving "take-off". The girls may face the bar at right-angles, or the upright, or an oblique approach may be used, with various grips on the bars. Similarly a swinging rope may be used, where the timing of just when to jump is important, as the rope needs to be caught at the peak of its swing before moving away from the vaulter ; this may be done at floor level, then with a gradual increase of height and distance, taking off from such apparatus as spring-boards, forms, box, horse or bars.

For flying off the apparatus forms may be used and whether the push comes from the feet, the hands or some other part of the body the awareness of the flight in the air is important before some other part of the body meets the ground. A low box, inclined or double forms may be used to get on in any way (which should be done well and as part of the sequence of the vault), but with the flying off stressed ; again the feet and arms are the most usual parts to come off from and the feet to land on. Such apparatus provides height leading up to that of the lowest horse and buck and should be used first, as apparatus needs raising gradually to maintain skill and therefore confidence.

Ropes may be used when the girls can swing well and can achieve a good height ; it is then possible to drop off at the peak of the swing either on the backward or the forward swing, the former is the easier. In both it is useful, at the peak of the swing, to get a good pull upwards to get the body vertical and the feet under the body ready to meet the ground ; then both hands should let go simultaneously. Confidence is needed to let go at the peak of the swing and ability in meeting the floor, as the pull of the swinging rope unbalances the performer if the timing is not correct and she should be prepared to meet the ground in an off-balanced way. The better the judgement of timing in this, the easier the landing. The ropes may be used in conjunction with a bar, as above, but passing over the bar. Ability and confidence are needed and it is better to have the bar too low to start with than too high — the girls themselves may be allowed to raise the bar when they feel able to try a greater height.

Large apparatus such as the horse and full box give more opportunity to experience flight, but it should be remembered that it will never be achieved, however high the apparatus, if the girls just drop off. They need to propel themselves upwards and it is that moment of suspension coming between their force upwards and the force of gravity downwards that is so important.

Thus it is possible to fly *onto* and *off* apparatus as separate tasks, but as the girls become skilled stress can be laid on the flying onto as well as the flying off the apparatus.

It is also possible to **fly along apparatus,** the direction stressed being forwards, whereas in flying on and off apparatus it is upwards and downwards. Some suggestions which start at floor level might include the use of a mattress, mats or forms used lengthways, going from the feet onto the hands as far along the apparatus as possible. The "take-off" may be a stationary or a moving one. Then the box can be used lengthways increasing the height as ability increases. The box is wider than the form and is padded so it is quite comfortable to land on with the whole body, which often happens in the initial stages, but this should not be encouraged.

The aim is to get flight along the length of the apparatus from the moment of "take-off" until the hands meet the apparatus at the far end. There are many ways of achieving this and time should be given to explore them and gain confidence and so skill. Movement suggestions may be made to help this exploration, such as, whether the body is curled or stretched and whether the legs are together or apart as they pass through the air. The girls might start in a forward direction and turn as they fly, ending facing the apparatus, at the side if they don't get right along, or at the end when they can achieve it. They may travel parallel to the apparatus, whether over it or out to the side or even upside-down over the length of it. If the horse is used, care should be taken that the horse is placed so that the hands are put onto the flat end of the horse and *not* the sloping end which might cause the vaulter to fall onto her head.

When experience has been given in covering the length of the apparatus in many ways, taking off from the feet, flying onto the hands on the apparatus, being curled, stretched, turning, passing over the apparatus or to either side in different ways, it can be made more daring and thrilling by the addition of a spring-board or a trampette, thus they have their own spring plus that of the spring-board, thus increasing the distance it is possible to cover. The spring-board can be moved further away from the apparatus or another piece of apparatus added to give greater length to the flight.

It is also possible to **fly over apparatus** where the vaulter does not touch the apparatus at all. The parts of the body receiving the weight will be either the legs, after some form of jump (which are strong and able to carry the weight safely from considerable height), or the arms followed by the shoulders and spine. The danger in the former will be in catching the feet on the apparatus after the "take-off" and during the flight, thus the height and width of apparatus must be increased very gradually according to the ability of the girls to spring and their confidence, and not what the teacher would hope for, which does sometimes happen. There is a real need here to be able to fall safely. If it is the arms which take the weight initially, the vaults take the form of "dives". It must be remembered that compared with the legs the arms are relatively weak. Again progression must be gradual and it is essential that the arms can and do take the weight with ease, because of the momentum and height of the full body weight falling onto them. Again, it is a good idea to start at floor level, perhaps diving over a saddle onto a mattress, at first with a stationary start, and later with a running "take-off" with gradual increase in the number of saddles and consequently the length of the flight. Then a low box might be used widthways ; here the height is being increased and can be raised by the addition of more lifts of the box. With a solid piece of apparatus, such as the box, the landing area cannot be seen and this sometimes puts the girls off ; if this is so, a low bar might be used and when the height of a horse is achieved this could then be used.

When the girls are skilled in flying onto, off, along and over apparatus it is possible to combine apparatus so that two or more of these experiences may be achieved in a vaulting sequence. Occasionally, with a good class, they may be allowed to work out, in small groups, their own apparatus and how it is to be arranged to give opportunity to achieve the task of flight.

Fig. 1. Weight transference using adjacent parts of the body.

(*Face page* 30)

Fig. 2. Weight transference using non-adjacent parts of the body.

FIG. 3. Weight transference involving flight.

FIG. 4. Weight transference using non-adjacent parts of the body on double bars. (The sequence begins on the right of the apparatus.)

Fig. 5. Flight onto hands
onto the apparatus.

Fig. 6. Flight onto feet
onto the apparatus.

at a time, therefore the bending and stretching of the spine will be dealt with first followed by that of the limbs.

In the bending and stretching of the spine the movement will be caused by the muscles of the trunk ; those in front of the spine, when contracting, will cause it to bend forwards. Those down the back on contracting will bring the spine to the upright causing it to stretch, and if these muscles go on contracting they will make the spine *bend* backwards, the head getting nearer to the heels : this often happens when the class and the teacher aim to achieve a full stretch but results in this bending backwards. This is then not a true stretching. The awareness of the relationship of the parts of the body one to another needs to be trained. There is no harm in bending backwards, in fact it should be taught, but the thing that matters is that the girl knows when she is stretching and when bending. This kinesthetic awareness is most important from a postural training point of view. Besides bending forwards and backwards the spine can also bend sideways.

These actions of bending and stretching, whatever the direction or level in space, with the body supported on various parts, take place round the centre of the body. The examples given below are used to illustrate the possible variations within the actual bending and stretching of the spine. Thus it is possible to move *both ends* of the spine towards the centre ; for example from lying on the back the shoulders and knees can be made to meet halfway, thus the movement starts in the centre drawing the two ends together. The *upper end* of the spine can be moved down towards the lower end, for example from lying on the back the head and shoulders can bend down towards the hips and knees. The pelvis being fixed the movement starts at the head end of the spine. If the *lower end* of the spine is moved up towards the upper end, for example from lying on the back, the knees and hips are curled up towards the shoulders — the movement starts at the lower end of the spine. In all these examples the same muscles are working, but in different ways with different effects on the body. Situations should be set where it is possible to experience all of these and to make the class aware of them and so gain control and mastery over their bodies. The example used involved bending forwards, but it also applies to all other directions. The body weight can be supported on a variety of parts, varying in size, therefore more or less stable ; for example the shoulders, hips, knees, one knee or hands. Sometimes the part of the body supporting the weight has to be bent in order to carry the weight, for example if on the knees, then they do not take part in the stretching.

The bending and stretching of the legs is most important as it happens whenever there is a meeting of the floor (where there is a bending) or going away from the floor (where there is a stretching) and occurs in all the joints.

Starting with the *movement in the hip joint*; bending forwards rarely causes trouble, but full stretching and bending backwards is often poor which results in loss of efficiency, which shows in such things as running, as though the knees were tied together. The thigh should be free to move backwards at the hip joint thus allowing a much longer length of stride. Girls can be made aware of this by experiencing such things as running with a wide space between the knees as against a small space ; stepping forwards and backwards small and large distances and so finding from experience what is involved and necessary to achieve a skilful action. Given such a task as "Find different ways of moving the legs backwards", the class can explore other possibilities by taking their weight on other parts of the body and discover movements involving this action by moving one or both legs backwards bringing the feet nearer to the head. The girls will have many ideas and it is for the teacher to observe and give them opportunity to experience each other's ideas, which may stimulate further ideas and will widen their vocabulary. To achieve skill and improvement the range of movement will need coaching.

Compensation for stiffness in the hip joints can be made if the spine is mobile, but here it is up to the teacher to observe and correct accordingly. If the girls understand what is being aimed at they are usually co-operative in achieving it. The use of swing to produce momentum is often helpful in this situation. A sideways movement of the thigh is also possible (abduction) and should similarly be explored.

Bending and stretching *at the knee joint* is possible and is most important, both when meeting the ground and again when jumping away from it. When meeting the ground after a jump the knees need to give and the amount of bending depends on the descent of the body, for example in jumping on the floor only a slight bending is necessary, but if from a height a full bending of the knees is essential and sometimes even followed by a transference of weight into a roll, to eliminate strain of muscle. In elevation the knees are often not fully stretched, indicating that the full power of the muscles has not been used. Girls can be guided to this discovery by comparing the height or distance covered when jumping off bent legs as against a fully stretched leg — this is simple to observe and should fairly easily be put right — children are often unaware that their legs are not straight and observation and the helping of each other is of great help and interest to the girls.

At the ankle joint bending and stretching is also essential in all forms of leaving and meeting of the floor. A stretched ankle should be the *result* of the strong push off by the muscles of the lower leg. If this is not used power is lost. Here again, as in the case of the knees, the girls can find the truth of this statement in a very practical way. At times girls can be seen jumping and then stretching the ankle because they have been told to "stretch their ankles", but it should be the outcome, due to the muscle contraction, and this lifts the body weight. Similar to the hip and knee joints the ankle should bend when meeting the ground.

Continuing down to the extremity of the leg the next joints

involved are those *at the ball of the foot* and these are the most neglected. The toes are small and often the muscles weak due to lack of use, perhaps through the continual wearing of shoes, and girls often jump or walk using the foot as a whole. In elevation the toes should be the last part of the body to leave the ground and therefore the last part to push off from, and full use of them should be encouraged to gain the maximum result. In meeting the ground it is the toes which should contact the floor first, working strongly to receive the weight of the body initially, the muscle tension gradually lessening and the joints giving, the movement passing up the leg through the ankle, knee and hip joints so preventing jarring and strain. So it can be seen how important stretching and bending is in all joints of the leg for good elevation and the meeting of the floor.

The bending and stretching of the arms comes into action when taking the weight of the body, whether supported or suspended from them. The arms are by no means as strong as the legs and it may be necessary to give work which will increase their strength so that the body weight can be carried by them with ease. Activities where the weight is *suspended* from the arms such as hanging and swinging on wallbars, ropes or bars with the lifting and lowering of the body : working with a partner or in three's *lifting* each other : where the arms *support* the body weight (it being transferred onto them) whether on the floor, onto low or onto higher apparatus or lowering the body from the apparatus to the hands which meet the floor first to take the body weight then gradually bending until the shoulders take the weight on the ground for a rolling recovery from the vault.

Besides being aware of what the Body is doing, the teacher must be aware of the Effort and Space involved. It is possible to put an equal stress on both the bending and the stretching when, from the point of view of the *Weight Factor*, the tension in the opposing muscle groups is alternately of equal strength, but this leads to a rather mechanical action. In most natural

actions there is a preparation leading to a main action and
then a recovery

// Preparation / Action / Recovery //

Thus the teacher needs to decide whether she needs to stress
the curling or the stretching and to use the other as a preparation ; for example if stressing the stretching, there should be
a preparatory curling which can be of a weak tension, gradually
increasing to a strong tension with the main action of stretching, reaching the maximum tension at full stretch, after which
there should be an immediate recoil, the body bending and
the tension becoming weaker. To make a sequence of movement the recovery of the first action may become the preparation for the following action.

//Preparation / Action / Recovery   / Action / Recovery //
                          Preparation

The stress can also be put on the bending, in a similar way,
with the stretching as the preparation and recovery.

The **Time Factor** also plays its part ; for example the
preparatory bending may be slower whilst the main stretching
is quicker. This interplay of quick and slow movement with
strong and weak tensions leads to resilience in movement.
In the same way other combinations of the strong and weak
tensions with the quick and slow speeds may be used, thus
the preparation might be quick and of a strong tension whilst
the main action is slow and of a weak tension. Opportunity
should be given to explore these possibilities and the various
resulting rhythms.

The **Space around the body** may be used in all directions
possible, whether forwards, backwards, sideways or up and
down, as well as the many in between. It is possible to bend
and stretch in the low level near to the floor or in the medium
and high levels which take one further away from the floor.
As previously mentioned the action may extend a short distance into space or take its full range going as far as is possible.

As bending and stretching is such a fundamental action and

occurs in most movement, it affords continual opportunity to be stressed and coached in movements and activities. Such actions as running ; running and jumping ; the making of jumping and stepping sequences involving long and short steps ; bending and stretching of the legs in all directions or moving about the gymnasium taking the body weight on different parts of the body and balancing momentarily, being aware of whether curled or stretched with varied Time and Weight changes. Small apparatus may be used such as hoops, canes or mats and, later, forms as obstacles to get through, over, under, along or onto, exploring the possibilities of bending and stretching. These are only a few situations which should lead to further ideas on the part of the teacher. The class can first explore the need for curling and stretching of the body in order to achieve an action, and then with coaching and help from the teacher can find further possibilities of curling and stretching and become more skilled in their execution and gain a greater vocabulary of movement. In these examples the whole of the body is in action (though there may have been a stress on a certain area) and transference of weight involved. The greater the number of different parts of the body used, the wider the use of Effort and Space and the greater the variety of situations given (where the task is fulfilled) will lead to greater movement experience. These situations might be used in the Introductory part of the lesson or as Class Activities.

The larger apparatus such as the box and horse may be used where the girls may get on and then come off with a stretch (curl) or go over the apparatus. Where there is length of apparatus they may go along stressing either the stretching or curling. At first the teacher might stress which aspects she wishes the class to achieve and later give them the choice. Similarly ropes and bars give opportunity to stress either or both of these fundamental actions.

CHAPTER VI

The Fundamental Body Action of Turning and Twisting

THIS, as are bending and stretching, is a fundamental action of the body due to the anatomical structure at the various joints. It is not possible to twist at every joint, but it is possible in the shoulder and hip joints and in the combined movement of the vertebrae of the spine.

It is difficult to separate twisting from turning for both are inter-related — we are all aware of turning the head to look over the shoulder, and this is really a *twist* or rotation of the head ; or for instance when walking suddenly changing one's mind and turning to return along the same pathway, here the twist occurs in the spine and hip joints, but we have *turned the whole body* to face the opposite way. In general movement when speaking of turning it seems rather concerned with twisting part of the body in order to bring part or the whole body to face another direction, the twist varying in degree, but rarely using the full range of movement in the joints involved. What then is involved when a twist occurs ? Taking the first example of turning, or more accurately twisting the head ; the shoulders remain still whilst the head turns to face a different direction. This situation may be repeated with many other parts of the body — the fundamental of fixing one part whilst another part twists to face a different direction.

Since we are dealing with the body as a whole in gymnastics and not isolation of parts of the body, the spine will most likely be involved. Thus if the lower half of the body is fixed by taking the weight on such parts as the feet, knees or hips, the upper half is free to twist. Similarly the reverse is possible — fixing the upper part by taking the weight on such parts as the arms or shoulders and twisting the lower half. Thus in twisting, one part of the body will face one way whilst the free part moves to face another direction. The fixing of the part of the body is most easily done by taking the body weight on that part, but it is also possible through pure muscle work, such as after a jump ; here the body is unsupported in the air and it is possible to twist before meeting the ground. This ability to twist the body gives it a pliability, movement becoming three dimensional, so leading to more varied and skilled movement and the ability to adapt to a variety of situations.

There are many ways of giving the experience of twisting the body or the feeling of one half screwing against the other. Unfortunately a popular way is standing on the feet or knees and turning the shoulders and head to face a different way and then returning along the same pathway. The twist has been experienced perhaps, and so far so good, but where has the movement led ? Nowhere ! because of the return along the same pathway. Situations are needed where the movement *continues*, leading to a transference of weight after that initial twist, which should be taken to the full extent before the transference of weight, to give flow and continuity to the action. Since transference of weight is involved it is perhaps better to take twisting with a class after they have some ability in transferring their weight in various ways (see Weight Transference).

Some suggestions where the experience of twisting may be given

Lying on the floor, stretched out, rolling over and over to ensure the feeling of continuous movement.

Repetition of the above but *both* shoulders are kept on the floor whilst the hips and lower half of the body are rolled over ; when the hips have twisted as far as possible the shoulders and upper half of the body should follow. This is done continuously. The reverse may also be done, moving the upper half first followed by the lower half. When the class has experienced this twisting in the spine and become aware of the need to fix one end and move the other to its maximum before the transference of weight, all types of twisted "rolls" (using adjacent parts of the body) may be explored with variations in the use of the body (curled or stretched), the use of directions and the Effort content.

The weight may be taken on the knees and one hand, and the head and one shoulder twisted under the supporting arm, in other words through the "hole" made by that arm and the floor. To get the maximum twist in the spine, it is the shoulder that needs to go through the hole made, and will come in contact with the floor ready to take the person's weight, then the hips will follow untwisting the spine as the body weight is transferred from the shoulder down the side of the body to the hips. Other "holes" may be made with different parts of the body and the floor, and different parts may lead and twist through.

Both of these examples are rather "earth bound", but if the class work in two's where No. 1 makes the hole and No. 2 twists through, it is possible to get further away from the floor. They should take it alternately, combining to make a continuous sequence, the twisting through leading into the making of a hole for the partner to use. It is necessary to stress the twist as it is possible to pass through a single hole without twisting. If two holes are used there is more opportunity given, but in either case co-operation and understanding by the class is essential.

Partners may join together holding one or both hands, taking it in turn to twist. This leads to co-operation between the two and involves skilled weight transference both near to the floor and further away from it, giving new movement experiences.

The body weight can thus be taken on any part of the body and the free half twisted to its maximum before the weight is transferred onto it which then leads to an unwinding of the body.

Whilst the experience of what the body is doing is being given, the class should also be made aware of the **Effort content** involved. The twist needs a strong tension in the muscles to produce the twist and to take it to its maximum (it is essential to get that extra final effort or else no progress will be made), also there needs to be a firm grip by the "fixed" part in contact with the floor (the fixing is only partially achieved by taking the body weight, the rest by the grip of the muscles). As the body weight is transferred over the receiving part of the body, the muscle tension is eased slightly, but then has to increase sufficient to resist the pull of gravity, releasing gradually to ensure a smooth meeting of the floor (see Weight Transference). Thus relatively the Action of the twist is of a stronger tension and the Recovery of a weaker tension. Variety may be achieved through the development of the Time Factor within the movement, thus the twist may be either quick or slow and the untwisting either slow or quick.

The experience of twisting may be given first as floor work and then used in activities and with apparatus. Also activities involving the need for a twist may be set, and the class seeing the need for the twist, may experience it on the floor, then return to the original activity with greater understanding and ability.

Some apparatus naturally encourages twisting, such as the Window Ladder ; a simple task of "Moving in and out of the holes" is likely to involve twisting. The holes can be used vertically, horizontally or obliquely, going up and coming down, leading either with the head or the feet. Similarly, horizontal Bars used in conjunction with the floor can be used ; the length of the bar "Continuously passing over and under" will involve twisting. One, two or three bars may be used according to the ability of the class.

Twisting may be used as a Movement task on such apparatus as forms, horse or box, but there the twisting is initiated by

Fig. 10. Twisting with the weight on different parts of the body.

CHAPTER VII

Awareness of the Body

THERE are ways of moving the body which may be stressed, in order to increase the awareness of the various parts, and of the parts to the whole. They will of necessity involve the fundamental movements of bending, stretching and twisting, due to anatomical structure, and the moving from one part of the body to another during transference of weight.

It is important that the body should move as a harmonious whole, but as is only natural we are more aware of certain parts of the body than of others and this may lead to a lack of ease of movement. It is possible to stress a part or an area of the body and so make the class more conscious of that part and its relationship to the rest of the body. The following are suggestions which may help a class to achieve greater awareness and mastery of their bodies.

1.   The **awareness of different parts of the body** may be stressed. The larger parts are accented first in simple ways when the class may be asked to move from one part to another, thus the girls become consciously aware of them. As their skill increases it will be found that smaller areas of the body may be used, for example one side of the seat instead of both, similarly with the shoulders, knees and feet, even the toes may take the weight rather than the whole foot. Different parts of the body such as the knees may be made to move alternately high and low. If there is a lack of awareness of an area of the spine, this may be stressed (see Chapter XVI) in whatever action is performed. Awareness of all parts of the body is important in all transference of weight (see Chapters II,

43

III and IV). To achieve a skilled and finished performance absolute awareness of the body is essential. Such questions as "Are the knees really straight?", "Should the feet be together or apart ?", "Is the head in alignment with the rest of the body ?" may help to achieve awareness of parts of the body and their relationship to the whole body. As the body is much involved in all movement one of the first things to teach is to be aware of it, but this goes on throughout with gradual deepening of awareness as skill and experience are gained.

2. The **awareness of the relationship** of one part to another **as in meeting and parting** may be taken when the girls are aware of the parts of the body. Besides knowing the parts involved there is a kinesthetic sense demanded in order that they meet accurately and the smaller the area chosen the more difficult. It is easier, for example, for a foot to be made to meet the shoulder than for the toe to meet the point of the shoulder.

To achieve movement involving the whole body, help may be needed in the selection of suitable parts in order to give full movement of the torso, and it helps to limit the choice to one part in the upper half of the body and the other to the lower half. Even so, it is possible to move very little as in the case of making the hand meet the knee ; however if it were the shoulder meeting the knee much more movement would result. When the class has understood what is required, the selection of suitable parts becomes part of the task. After this selection has been made the girls should move the two parts towards and away from each other, exploring the different pathways of movement possible ; so bending, stretching and twisting forwards, backwards and sideways will be used, especially if the girls are encouraged not to return along the same pathway. Other Space aspects which may be developed are those of Extension Levels, Central and Peripheral movement (see Chapter XI). Transference of weight onto various parts of the body should take place throughout the movement and the level will vary according to the part of the body taking the weight. Variation in Effort content, particularly of the Weight, Time and Flow Factors, should be encouraged and developed in similar ways as used in Bending, Stretching, Twisting and Weight Transference, giving resilience and rhythm to the sequences.

Awareness of the relationship of one leg to the other may be taught in the Introduction of a lesson using stepping, running or jumping in various ways. The relative size of the step bringing the feet nearer or further apart ; jumping with feet really together or apart ; the moving of one leg away from the other rather than moving both, are just a few examples. These basic relationships of one part to another will gain in variety through the use of the various aspects of Space and Effort content.

3. Awareness of the body may be increased further by making a **part of the body important** involving a variety of ways of using the part selected. It will be important if it leads the movement, or it may be that the part is used to take the body weight, to lift or elevate the body into the air, to swing it or move it in different directions or levels. The girls may select a part of the body themselves, or the teacher may stipulate which part they are to emphasise. As in other cases the smaller the part chosen the greater the concentration and skill demanded. For example the legs may be made important when they may be used to step, run, jump, gesture, to swing with an accent in some direction or to lead the body, but if it is the toes which are to be stressed the movement will have to extend right down the leg to the very extremity and so will demand greater skill and awareness.

With this theme the same part of the body may be stressed throughout the lesson in the different situations or different parts may be chosen according to the needs of the class, though the former will, of course, give greater stress and therefore awareness of the one selected area.

4. The awareness of one **part of the body leading** the movement is another possibility. This is quite different, for the operative word is leading. This means that the rest of the body must follow and this is only possible to the extent of the range of movement that that particular part can travel, when the direction must be changed, which may increase the pathway, but soon a time comes when another suitable part of the body must take over the lead to ensure continuity of movement. Continual transference of weight is essential with anticipation of the various parts of the body to take the lead to obtain rhythm and flow of movement.

This theme may be used successfully throughout the lesson both as floor work and with apparatus with girls with movement ability and can add greatly to the precision, clarity and flow of their movement, but with classes who have had little movement experience it can result in a mere sticking out of a part of the body, which is not profitable.

5. The body is formed **symmetrically** having a right and a left side, therefore both may move in a similar way. However, few people use both sides equally with the same skill, but perform definite actions with a favourite side and so movement may be **asymmetrical.** Development of skill and awareness of moving the body symmetrically as well as asymmetrically should be deepened, though the natural tendency of the individual will always remain.

To move symmetrically, making the right and left sides of the body do exactly the same at the same time, requires considerable self-discipline : jumping off both feet ; making the legs move in the same way ; both sides of the torso ; in meeting the ground whether it be with the feet, knees, hands or shoulders. On exploring the possibilities of moving the spine, besides both sides of the body being used similarly, it will be found that it is only possible to move forwards, backwards and up and down, and so there is a Spacial as well as a Body discipline. This limitation in the use of the Body and the

Space gives rise to actions of a very stable nature, thus symmetrical movement tends to be more on-balance than asymmetrical movement.

Asymmetrical movement is far less limiting and there are many possibilities where the two sides of the body are used differently, involving bending and stretching in all directions, twisting and turning with unequal take off and meeting the ground. The smaller the part of the body taking the weight the more noticeable is the mobility of the action which is characteristic of this way of moving. When moving asymmetrically it is a good thing to stress the right and then the left sides of the body or else the girls will only use the favourite side and so their movement experience will be limited, particularly in such actions as jumping off one foot, rolling over one shoulder or always twisting to the same side. This is important for a balanced movement training, and in certain situations it is necessary to move using the less natural side of the body.

This theme may be used as floor work, using low apparatus, working with a partner and finally on the large apparatus. Since all movement has to be one or the other, the task should set which aspect the teacher requires to be stressed. To ask a class to "Move sometimes symmetrically and sometimes asymmetrically" will result in them moving with complete freedom as all movement falls into one category or the other. A better task might be "Move and at some point stress moving symmetrically". This would draw their attention and concentration onto the symmetrical part of the sequence. Similarly when using apparatus the task needs to be quite definite, for example, "Get on symmetrically".

6. The joints of the body may be moved **simultaneously** or **successively**. In the former the movement in every joint involved happens at the same time. In successive movement the action starts in one joint and then when almost complete passes to the adjacent joint and so on through the body, each joint moving in succession, leading to a ripple of movement

through the body. When more than one joint is involved, either way is possible, and girls should be made aware of this and given opportunity to experience the different muscle co-ordination involved. When bending the spine it is possible to move both ends of it towards the centre, all joints moving simultaneously ; it is also possible to fix one end of the spine and move the other towards it, joint by joint, when the action is successive. When transferring the weight from one base to another, the action is simultaneous if the weight of the body falls directly over the base, all joints giving to receive it ; but if the body weight is drawn part by part over the support the action is successive. Such an occasion might be when swinging on a rope and dropping vertically (letting go just at the right moment) onto the feet onto a box of medium height, the joints of the legs giving simultaneously : but if the vaulter's feet lead, reaching forward ahead of the arms and body towards the box, the feet meet the box first and the rest of the body, part by part, is drawn over the feet, and a wave of movement passes successively through the body.

On the whole more simultaneous movement occurs in gymnastics than successive, but there are times when the one is more appropriate than the other and both should be experienced and the possibilities explored. It often occurs during transference of weight from the upper to the lower part of the body as when recovering from a backward bend when the knees straighten first followed by the spine, bringing the body to the upright, or going forward under a bar of hip height, where the feet lead followed by the knees, hips, chest and finally the head.

CHAPTER VIII

The Way (or How) a Person Moves — Effort Content

So far stress has been put on the body — in fact *what* moves — the arms, legs, spine or the whole body ; what part is being used to take the weight ; what is stretching or twisting ; but there is more to movement than that, as may have been realised, as Effort content has been mentioned in direct relationship to the various body actions : it is the Effort content which makes movement possible.

Besides asking oneself what is being moved, one can ask the question *how* is the movement carried out ? Such questions might be "Is it quickly ? slowly ? gently ? or with great strength ? " In the following chapters will be discussed the factors which influence how actions may be performed.

When a person moves, energy is used and the various forms of energy have been called Effort by Rudolf Laban, on whose principles this work is based. If a person moves suddenly or with sustainment she has a certain attitude towards Time ; firmly or gently an attitude towards Weight ; directly or flexibly an attitude towards Space and with bound or free flow an attitude towards Flow. These attitudes towards Time, Weight, Space and Flow, Laban called the Motion Factors — things which influence how a movement is carried out.

Every individual has her own instinctive way of moving and therefore may be more naturally able with certain aspects of Effort content than others, and consequently have some limitation in movement ; it is for the educationist to give opportunity for the class to experience the whole width of movement. The individual can then select the most suitable for any task, which we hope will make her more adaptable and able to deal with unfamiliar situations more easily, due to her width of ability and understanding. When teaching, the teacher should observe the girls and see what is lacking or in excess in their movement, and so guide them accordingly, thus the skill required should improve rapidly. This Effort analysis, which is common to all movement, should be used in all aspects of Physical Education so that the girls can, through their intelligence and the consistency of the teacher, transfer the experiences gained in one type of lesson to another.

The factors of Time, Weight, Space and Flow are present in all movement in varying degrees. In some actions there is a stress on one and in others a different stress, but very often and much the most usual, there is an interplay which gives rhythm to the action — a resiliency and fluency of movement — which gives to the performer the satisfaction of something done well, yet using the minimum of energy, and to the on-looker the action looks easy.

In gymnastics we are very much involved with the functional, the objective or practical use of these Factors, but since we are dealing with human beings who have minds and feelings as well as bodies, it is impossible to separate this practical side entirely from the sensation side of movement. Both the action and the movement sensation produced are always present. In gymnastics the stress is on the practical action, though at times movement sensation is experienced, whereas in dance the stress is on the expressive or movement sensation, though the practical use of the body is not neglected. Each Factor has its extremes which Laban named the Elements of movement ; the one, in which one may fight against, and the other in which one yields, or indulges. Similarly, each Element has its practical aspect as well as its movement sensation. Each of the Factors of Weight, Time, Space and Flow will be discussed in turn.

THE WEIGHT FACTOR

The Weight Factor is concerned with the various tensions in the muscles which move the body and the resulting movement sensations caused. In order to move at all there has to be muscle contraction, therefore the Weight Factor is inevitably involved in every action, it is the most practical of all the Factors ; and there is the continual fight against gravity to maintain the upright position which involves varying degrees of tension, and without this, gravity takes over and the person is said to be "giving way to weight".

If one fights against Weight a resistance is set up and the Element is called Firm, when yielding to Weight the Element is called Gentle or Fine Touch.

The practical aspect of the **Firm Element** concerns the **strong tension** in the muscles, and the body is powerful, which enables it to move lesser or greater distances in various directions according to the power or tension in its muscles. It is also able to lift, carry or move external objects. Since this is a very real physical contraction of muscle fibres, the primary sensation is probably a kinesthetic one ; a feeling of physical power, able to resist or fight, a **weighty** "down to earth" and stable feeling. Linked very much with this are the characteristics of grit, determination and strength of mind.

The practical aspect of the Element **Gentle or Fine Touch** is when the tension in the muscles is **weak,** varying from just sufficient to combat gravity and to keep the body actively moving, to a degree of strength which then enters the realms of strong tension. If the tension is lessened beyond this weak tension there is a flabbiness of the body and it moves lethargically in an over relaxed way — a giving way — so that in part, gravity takes over. True Gentle movement requires just enough tension to cancel out the pull of gravity. This minimum tension makes it possible to be more aware of the sensation side to the Element which is one of lightness, of being airborne, a **weightlessness,** of being lifted or supported by the air.

Since gymnastics is involved with the moving of the body, the Weight Factor is of primary importance as will have been realised from the chapters on Weight Transference. People move and therefore use their muscles, but the skill of movement, which is judged by the ease with which they move, is very dependent on the fine adjustment of muscle tensions. How much tension is needed at this particular moment? These tensions vary according to the situation and from individual to individual, and it is only after much practice that ease of movement is achieved. As the judgement and ability of the individual improves actions will become skilled in less and less time. The teacher can help, for she should know where stronger or relatively weaker tension is necessary, but after the girls have an intellectual understanding, opportunity to put it into practice is essential; the girls need time for repetition of action, to make their muscles respond — not mere repetition, but repetition with growth of skill.

The extremes of strong and weak tensions are necessary and can be extended further, but they are useless without the smooth transition from one to the other to achieve a resilient fluency of movement. With ability in the use of the varying degrees of tension one becomes aware of the rhythm of the movement, its accent and recovery from the main action, which is often the preparation for the next action. There should be this rhythm in ALL Movement, not just when meeting the floor and bouncing away from it when landing on the feet, which is often a mistaken conception.

Present day civilisation, due to the trend towards mechanisation, is making us less aware of the rhythms of the human body, which were so common in the working actions of the past. One had only to watch a farmer with his scythe, the woodcutter with his axe or the road mender with his pick to appreciate the economy of effort due to the interplay of muscle tensions. Gradually these natural rhythms are being lost and we are getting less conscious of them, which is affecting the movement of everyday life, they are getting ironed out, dull, less efficient and casual. In gymnastics it is possible to maintain and develop this inborn sense of rhythm in a very practical way and perhaps it is the rhythms of the Weight and Time Factors which are the most fundamental.

The awareness of degrees of tension is so essential, it being impossible to move without them, that it is most important to teach them alongside and with the use of the body (see chapters on Weight Transference, Bending and Stretching and Twisting). In presenting lessons to a class it is possible to have the main stress on the use of the body, but it is the Effort content which makes it possible to achieve and therefore the teacher must be aware of what is involved. The main stress may also be put on the Effort content, in which case a subsidiary known use of the body may be used, the main coaching point being that of the variations of tension involved.

Some suggested activities where the various tensions may be coached

All movement involving transference of weight, whether using adjacent or non-adjacent parts of the body (see Weight Transference). In both, there is an interplay, though the latter uses greater tension than the former due to the distance the body weight has to be moved.

All actions involving flight require interplay of even greater tensions, as for example in jumping, where in order to leave the ground strong tension is needed to lift the body into the air, then it is released to just sufficient to maintain the upright, when the jumper should have the experience of being suspended in the air (this is often lost due either to over tension or insufficient tension), then there is an increase of tension in the legs, the toes meeting the ground first, taking the weight and releasing quickly but smoothly, to bring the balls of the feet, then the heels to the ground with the bending of ankles, knees and hips, followed again by a strong increase of tension to lift the body again to standing. In the meeting of the floor, if the strong tension is maintained there is a hardness, a jarring and bruising ; the lack of or too rapid a release of tension results in a floppiness. Judging just the right amount of tension comes from understanding and much repetition, varying with the weight of each girl and the distance between her body and the floor.

All movement sequences should have a Weight rhythm where there is accent and recovery, whatever the aspect taken on which to base the sequence. For example, in a sequence of Twisting the twist may be accented and the untwisting will be the recovery ; in which case the twist should involve stronger tensions and the recovery weaker, giving an interplay.

Low apparatus such as forms may be used involving various ways of transferring the weight. The higher over the apparatus the body is lifted, the greater the strength needed. A rhythmic sequence may be achieved from such a task as "Moving alternately close to the apparatus and far from it".

Similarly, variety in the heights of obstacles gives opportunity to become aware of the difference in tension required to get on and off from them. In the same way shorter and longer distances to be covered involve varying degrees of tension.

Besides lifting and manipulating one's own weight it is possible to lift, partially or completely, another person's weight ; as when working with a partner at such a task as "Helping a partner to get high". Here the supporting partner must judge where and when her force must be applied, and the stronger the tension she uses, the higher will she be able to send her partner.

Experience of tension may be felt in all hangings, swingings, liftings and lowerings of the body using such apparatus as bars and ropes. The body weight may be carried completely by part of the body or distributed between two or more parts. In all cases strong tension is needed to grip the apparatus whether it be with hands, elbows, knees or feet, and opportunity should be given to discover what parts of the body it is possible to grip with and at the same time support the hanging body : a weaker tension is required in the rest of the body to prevent it becoming "sack-like". Changing from hanging on one part to another gives the experience of alternating strong tension in different parts of the body, with the release in others ; thus one might hang from a high bar by the arms, lower the body to a lower bar and hang from this by the knees. Momentum may be developed in conjunction with the tensions in various activities leading to swinging. The development of various directions and orientations of the body in the space gives variety and agility.

When using apparatus such as a box or horse there is often the need to change from the maximum tension in part of the body to the maximum tension in another with the release in the first part used. This often needs bringing to the notice of the girls and practice is required to achieve the right interplay of tensions to give true resilience to the vault.

Judgement is needed as to the correct tension required to achieve the best results ; too much is unnecessary and the action tense, too little and the task is not achieved, the body being over relaxed : degrees of tension need to be used objectively so that the body moves with ease — it is pointless just to "make part of the movement strong and part less strong".

The sensation of weightlessness, of being airborne or suspended in the air (whether supported or unsupported as in flight) is made possible by the changing from a greater tension (which gets the body there) to a lesser tension (just sufficient to maintain the body in action and counter the pull of gravity) when the sensation side of the Element may become uppermost.

CHAPTER IX

The Time Factor

THE contrasting Elements are **Sudden** and **Sustained**. Fighting against Time gives a sudden movement whereas if one yields or indulges in Time the result is a sustained movement.

The practical side of the Elements may be described as moving with **Quick** or **Slow** speeds, which can be measured, as in fact is so often done in races — who arrives most quickly at the winning post ? Who was the slowest ? The movement sensations experienced with these Elements have with the one a feeling of **momentariness,** a bursting, taking no time, all over before it has started and it is the arrival that matters; as contrasted to the sensation of **endlessness,** lingering, an awareness of the slow passage of time and it is the going that matters.

To illustrate the point that in practical situations it is the measurable side of the Element that dominates, but the movement sensation is present, take the athlete who is running a hundred yards sprint. He prepares himself for the start and as the gun is fired he bursts away. The burst is a momentary experience and then he runs as quickly as he can to the winning post. That start to the race was more than a physical thing which he experienced, but later it was a physical battle against time. In the gymnasium there are similar moments ; such as the run up for a vault, which gradually quickens, the speed increasing to the moment to "take off", which is momentary, and the vaulter is in the air before she realises, having experienced the feeling or sensation of bursting away from the ground. Often only the material or more mechanical side of actions is considered, and the teacher wonders what is lacking, perhaps it is this other side which gives life and vitality to action.

Girls should be given the opportunity and helped to experience both sudden and sustained movement. It is easier if
stimulated by the teacher, who may use her voice, so setting
the rhythm and providing the external stimulus ; it is more
difficult for the girls to initiate it themselves, the stimulus and
rhythm coming from them, but the latter is of greater value.
Moving quickly and slowly is a beginning, but the smooth
transition from one to the other is more difficult especially
if one follows the other rapidly — these transitions are most
important and help to give fluency and resilience of movement.

Some suggestions where Time changes may be experienced

Running gradually increasing speed and slowing down
either to command or initiated by the individual. Running
slowly and then a burst of speed using a common rhythm
or an individual one.

Transference of weight using other non-adjacent parts such
as the hands and feet in various ways moving slowly, then as
quickly as possible.

Jumping sequences where some jumps are done relatively
slowly and others more quickly giving a Time rhythm (the
Weight Factor is also involved).

Any movement of the body involving the spine, where
again the rhythm of quicker and slower movement is possible.
There are definite moments when the action is easier when
performed more quickly or more slowly and girls should be
allowed to explore and find out what is best for them, the
teacher being prepared to guide them to a right conclusion
if necessary, from her observation of their movement ; for
example, "In transferring the weight from the seat along the
spine to the shoulders and then onto the feet" ; it is easy to
roll down the spine quite slowly, but to get from the shoulders
onto the feet it is much easier for most girls if they move
more quickly — here the speed of movement assists the
strength of muscle work involved (see chapter on Weight
Transference using adjacent parts). Besides finding what

rhythm is best for oneself it is beneficial to all in the class to experience the opposite rhythm, in order to widen their movement vocabulary, though it would not have been their normal choice.

When using simple apparatus, such as mats or forms, it is possible to move along (using the body in any way) as quickly, then as slowly, as possible. Here the use of the body may be different in each case, but the girls are aware of the difference in the time taken to get along the apparatus. If the body is used in the same way first quickly and then slowly, the girls become even more aware of the difference in speed of the actual movement. When aware of the contrasts the girls may change at will from one to the other. This will develop a rhythmic interplay within the whole sequence and the transition from one to the other should be smooth whatever its length ; the shorter it is, the more difficult, and practice should be given in varied situations.

With large apparatus, where greater height and width are involved, careful thought is needed if tasks stressing the Time Factor are involved, both from the danger point of view and whether it is profitable or even possible. In order to get onto or over the reasonable height of apparatus a certain attack is needed and therefore sudden movement, so to set a task of "Get on and off slowly" would in many cases hardly be sensible — only leading to crawling onto and off the apparatus, which happens far too often. There are exceptions, of course, and it is possible to get onto lower apparatus relatively slowly, depending on the approach, the part of the body contacting the apparatus, and the following action. In getting off the apparatus there is gravity to contend with, over which we have little control if elevation is involved, but if there is a direct transference of weight it is possible to vary the speed. When moving along the apparatus there is more scope for Time changes, and then it is possible to say "Go along as slowly (quickly) as possible". Perhaps a better way of developing the Time changes is to start from the action task of "Go along the apparatus", then where the movement is slow, to make it slower, and where quick to make it quicker. This will deepen the natural rhythm of the vaulter and will make the girl think and concentrate on what she is doing, making her more aware of her own movement and so able to clarify. This gives scope for individual variations and characteristics, and widens the rhythmic experience of the girls if they try each other's sequences.

Knowledge of the ability of the class is needed, combined with good observation by the teacher, before she should demand any movement to be carried out quickly. If the girls are not absolutely safe, extreme quick movement may lead to accidents. When a task "to move quickly" is set, simple actions and activities with which the girls are familiar should be chosen or alternatively they may be allowed to select their own ways in which to move quickly.

The aim is for the teacher to give the girls the experiences of sudden and sustained movement, with its quick and slow action and momentary experiences of the sensations involved; then to interplay their use, leading to ease and fluency. The abrupt change from sudden to sustained, or vice versa leads to jerky movement and so loses fluency.

When deepening the use of the Time Factor in relation to any sequence of movement (which consists of Preparation, Action and Recovery) and the Action is sudden, the Preparation and Recovery will most likely be sustained and vice versa, the change or transition from one extreme to the other being gradual and smooth. The more able the girls become at these Time changes the more able they will be in movement — much practice is needed in many and varied situations.

RESILIENCE OF MOVEMENT

By resilience of movement is meant the rhythm or interplay of the Weight and Time Factors — the selection and achievement of just the right tension and speed to fulfil the task most economically. It applies to *all* movement whether it involves the meeting of the floor or not.

Although it may be necessary to make girls concentrate, at first, on the degrees of tension and speed separately, it is very difficult to keep them apart for long, as they help and assist each other ; for example — the run up for a vault involves the increase of tension and speed up to the moment of "take off", which may need maximum tension and speed to achieve the required height ; both are essential. An unsuccessful approach and "take off" may be due to lack of increase of both, or of either one of the Factors. In this example a strong tension is combined with a quick speed, which often happens in jumping ; but there are occasions when a strong tension may be combined with a slow speed of moving, as happens when the body is lowered slowly from such a piece of apparatus as a bar. Practice should be given with all possible combinations of the Weight and Time Factors — some tasks will necessitate one combination and others another ; some girls may achieve a movement through using a greater tension, whilst others might use a greater speed, and yet both be equally skilled. Individuals should be given full opportunity to find their own variations, and it is up to the teacher to observe and perhaps guide the individual towards what is right for her in that particular situation. Of course it is good to experience each other's rhythms and ways of moving to ensure a wide experience, it also helps one to select what is best for oneself.

Throughout it is necessary to remember that it is the interplay of the Weight and Time Factors which gives resilience to the movement, with the smooth change or transition from the fighting to the indulging aspect of the Factors ; and in all harmonious rhythmic movement there is a Preparation leading to the main Action followed by a Recovery, which in turn may be the preparation for the next action. A simple movement may be shown thus :

//Preparation / Action / Recovery //

An example of how the Weight Factor might be involved could be :

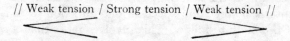

// Weak tension / Strong tension / Weak tension //

The length of Preparation, Action and Recovery may be varied at will, or may be directly influenced by the situation. However, the more skilled the performer the greater her ability to shorten the Preparation and still achieve the climax of the Action.

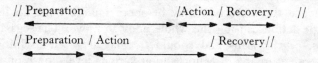

// Preparation   /Action / Recovery   //

// Preparation / Action   / Recovery//

A more complicated sequence where the Weight Factor is used in a similar way, with the addition of the awareness of the Time Factor might be :

Preparation	Action (1st)	⎰ Recovery ⎱ ⎱ Preparation ⎰	Action (2nd)	Recovery	– Sequence
Weak	Strong	Weak	Very strong	Weak	– Weight
Slow	Quick	Slow	Very quick	Slow	– Time

Where there is more than one Action within a sequence, one should be accented more than the others giving a climax within the movement ; in this example it is the second action which is the climax of the sequence.

Much practice is needed to recapture and deepen this natural rhythm of movement, but if girls once become aware of the accents within their movement sequences, they will move rhythmically and with greater ease.

A theme for a lesson which stresses the interplay of the Weight and Time Factors with the necessary transitions might be that of "Accented swing", where part of the body, not supporting the body weight (usually the upper or lower half according to the situation), swings and builds up sufficient momentum of force and speed in one direction to cause the rest of the body to follow. This involves more than a swing, which moves equally in two opposite directions, but accented (through the growth in Weight and Time) in one direction and when built up sufficiently the rest of the body is forced to follow in that same direction. At first it may be necessary to travel to and fro along the same pathway more than once, gradually extending it, due to the build up of the impetus, until sufficient to cause a transference of weight; with experience the crescendo may be more rapidly built up in a single action causing the whole body to move. The legs and hips, or the arms and shoulders, may be used to initiate movement in any direction and at various levels, both on the floor and on apparatus, the unsupported or free half of the body being ready to initiate the next action after the recovery from the first.

CHAPTER X

The Space and Flow Factors

The Space Factor

The Space Factor, as have the Weight and Time Factors, has two aspects involving, on the one hand, the movement sensation and on the other the objective function. It is the latter with which we are mainly concerned in gymnastics. The Elements of the Space Factor are those of **Directness** when fighting Space and **Flexibility** when indulging in the use of Space. The practical side of Directness is that of straightness, when the pathway is limited on all sides except in the direction travelled — an economy in the use of the space, travelling directly towards the goal. The practical aspect of Flexibility is that of waviness giving a roundabout or twisted pathway through the space, using the space in all directions three dimensionally.

· Much of the movement in the gymnasium tends to use the Element of Directness — directness of purpose and of action, whether taking a straight or curved pathway through the space as in bending, stretching, jumping, climbing and the getting on and off or over apparatus. When the body twists and turns a wavy or twisted pathway using the Element Flexibility is used. This can be observed in any twisting with weight transference on the floor or apparatus ; in initiating swinging movements with the upper or lower half of the body or in moving continuously over, under and round obstacles, but the pathway taken is of secondary importance resulting from the body action. If the stress is laid on the pathway through the space there is a tendency to lose sight of the practical aspect and the expressive side of the Elements becomes the most important leading to such criticisms as "dancing on the apparatus". The Space Factor in gymnastics is less consciously stressed, though at times the teacher may be able to help the individual by referring to it, using it as a subsidiary coaching point.

The Flow Factor

The Flow Factor has the Elements of **Bound** and **Free** Flow where there is a fighting against or an indulging in the Flow of movement. The movement sensation of Bound Flow is a withholding, restraint, a carefulness ; whilst the practical aspect is manifested in the ability to stop at any moment. The movement sensation of Free Flow is that of fluency in movement and the practical side that of going.

In gymnastics we are concerned with both the stopping and the continuous flow of movement, but a skilled mover experiences considerable sensation as a result of the practical actions.

Free Flow in movement may be achieved whether the body is on or off balance. In on-balance movement Free Flow is more difficult and is achieved through the interplay of the Time and Weight Factors giving a resilience and ease to sequences by the intermittent recharging of the energy resulting in one action flowing easily onto the next. When the body is off-balance or is flying or falling it is easier, as it is quite impossible to stop the movement. If the class find difficulty in achieving the "going" of movement these off-balance situations may put them into situations where it is impossible not to experience it momentarily (see chapters on Weight Transference, On- and off-balance, and Flight). With experience this originally rather abandoned, exaggerated Free Flow becomes skilled and the gymnast becomes aware of the movement and its fluency, experiencing a definite sensation which gives great satisfaction to the performer for it is now under her control. Such experiences may be given to a class using such themes as "On- and off-balance", "Accented swing", "Making a part of the body important" or "Flight". The earlier the better for a class to become aware of the fluency of Flow in its training, though full achievement will not be reached until good weight transference and adjustment of the body weight are mastered.

Younger classes who have not lost the "joy of moving" with its fluency should be helped to maintain it, by sound training in weight transference and the ability to manipulate their bodies with safety — they have the urge to move and the energy — this is the time to establish this flow of movement with the resulting satisfaction gained. It sometimes happens that a lively daring class fling themselves wildly at apparatus with exaggerated Free Flow. This can be dangerous and lead to accidents, but with help they can become masters of the Flow of movement.

The practical aspect of **Bound Flow** or the ability to stop or restrain movement also has its place in gymnastics. It is involved whenever the body is brought to a stillness, whether on the floor, working with a partner or on apparatus : in the careful lifting, lowering and placing of one's own body or that of a partner, here the body moves continuously but throughout with care and restraint. The anticipation of this stopping or placing requires a certain withholding of the flow of movement : a carefulness to prevent it going too far or too quickly involving a fine adjustment of the body weight and the whole Effort content of movement. Overstress on this aspect can lead to overcarefulness or a series of positions linked by little movement. Exploration is necessary to find the parts of the body on which it is possible to bring movement to a stillness and as experience and ability increase smaller parts are found possible to use. In all cases the body has to be on-balance at this point, the force of gravity falling through the base. Thought and practice should then be given to ways in which the flow may be bound, such as that of a gradual stopping of the action, or a sudden arrival and stop, where the position is held momentarily. With a theme of "Flow" or "Going and Stopping", the moments of stopping will easily form climaxes within a sequence of movement, but it is not good to have too many and guidance may be needed in selecting the most appropriate place to bind the flow of the movement whether it be on the floor or a sequence on the apparatus.

The skilled gymnast should have the ability to control the flow of her movement whether it be to move with fluency or to withhold and bind the flow. If it gets beyond her control it is exaggerated Free Flow and dangerous.

CHAPTER XI

The Use of Space

PREVIOUS chapters have suggested ways in which the body can move and how it is the Effort content which causes the movement to take place giving it resilience and rhythm, and in this chapter will be discussed *where* the body can move. The space is the medium of movement and whenever there is action it is used, whether on a stationary base or whether locomotion is involved.

1. *Personal Space*

Rudolph Laban spoke of the "sphere of movement" by which he meant the immediate space surrounding the body ; the outer limits being reached by stretching as far as possible in all directions and at all levels. It is within this **sphere of movement or Personal Space** that one moves without travelling, as though encased in a globe, its size depending on the extension of the body. The orientation of the body, within, always remains the same, the front always being the front. When travelling or turning, the sphere of movement is carried or turned accordingly, the body always being in the centre of it. Since we always have to move within this "sphere" it is necessary to become familiar with its extent at all levels and in all directions, and the different ways in which it is possible to move within it. Due to our anatomical structure and orientation it is very much easier to move in front of ourselves ; our eyes are directed forwards, as are our arms and legs, and it is more usual to use the legs at a low level and the arms at a high level, but it is possible to move in the less familiar areas using the space behind and to the side,

the legs in the upper area and the upper part of the body
in the lower area.

2. *General Space*

Besides becoming aware of the Personal Space around oneself it is also necessary to become conscious of the relationship
with other people or the use and sharing of the **General
Space — the space of the room** — in order to avoid col-
lisions, for when travelling off the spot one penetrates into
the General space. At one time in gymnastics, girls stood in
lines or on a definite spot on the floor and stayed there, thus
only moving within their own personal sphere of movement.
Now they are continually moving from one base to another
in different ways and this sense and judgement of the General
Space must be developed. The greater the floor space available the more each girl may take, but if the area is limited
it is amazing how skilled girls get in judging the area necessary
for their movement. They also learn to adapt their movement
to the area available at that moment by reducing it in size or
by changing the direction or level of the movement. This
continual awareness of others in the General Space with the
adaptation of their movement within their own Personal Space
serves them well in everyday life, for they become more adept
when moving through a crowd of people or avoiding obstacles
where such judgement is required.

When observing a group of girls moving, it is often found
that the more confident and secure they are, the more space
they will use if it is available. It is the self-conscious and insecure who crowd together fearing to be alone. Besides helping
girls to use the available space it is also important to help them
to gain confidence to move alone and so gain in independence.

3. *Directions in Space*

There are perhaps ways of thinking of the directions in
space, which lead to an awareness of the whole. The one

where the **body turns taking its Personal Space with it,**
so that the same surface of the body continually leads the way :
if facing and travelling North, for example, then by making
a quarter turn facing and moving forwards towards the East
or West, and then another quarter turn facing forwards and
travelling to the South. This involves a turn of the whole
body with its Personal Space, always moving with the same
body surface leading, but towards different points of the
compass. This is also possible, of course, with the back always
leading or the right or left sides of the body as well as the
front, though the latter is the most usual.

The other use of the directions in space is when the body
with its Personal Space does *not* turn but the front of the
body remains facing the same way: in other words the
orientation of the body in the space remains the same, and
as the body moves forwards, backwards, sideways or up and
down the different surfaces of the body lead the way in turn.
For example, if travelling North the front may lead and with
a change of direction to South the back would lead and to
East and West the right and left sides respectively. In gymnastics this use of the Space Directions gives rise to a great
variety of movement.

Space is three-dimensional and so is the human body,
having height, width and breadth. It is these three dimensions
which give us the six main directions of up and down, forwards and backwards and side to side. The directions radiate
from the centre of the body within the sphere of movement,
forming what is often referred to as the Dimensional Cross.
Girls should become familiar with these directions changing
at will from one to the other whether movement is on the
spot or involves travelling. In between these main directions
are many others and opportunity should be given to find the
many combinations of these main directions such as, forwards
and sideways or upwards, sideways and backwards.

In whatever way the body is being moved the possibilities
of the use of the different directions should be explored ; for

example the body can bend, not only forwards (which is the most usual) but sideways and backwards, thus moving the spine in all directions. Due to our anatomical structure it is usually easier to move forwards when transferring the weight, but there are times when it is essential to move in a sideways, backwards, upwards or downwards direction, so experience should be given and the more familiar the girls become with the less used directions the more versatile they will be in movement. The change from one direction to another involves an adjustment of the body weight which was discussed in the chapter on Weight Transference and so must be anticipated. This ability to move with ease in all directions demands skill in body management and an awareness of where one is in the space around.

When the body maintains the same orientation in the space there is a direct relationship between the directions and the surfaces of the body, but if the same direction is maintained it is also possible to lead with various parts of the body as can be seen in an action such as running in a northerly direction, for example, at first forwards, then backwards. This change also occurs when rolling, the different surfaces of the body taking the lead in turn. The awareness of the body whilst moving in the different directions and the linking of one with the other will help to clarify movement content and precision.

When using apparatus girls will soon achieve such a task as "Get on and off", but more will be demanded from them if asked to "Get on sideways" or "Get on backwards". When stressing the use of directions in conjunction with apparatus the height and width must be borne in mind. If the apparatus is low and narrow (Form) it is possible to get on forwards with a jump, but if it is high and narrow (three forms high) in which case the hands may be needed to assist, it is very much more difficult to get on forwards as the area of support is small for both the hands and the feet. In this case it might be easier to get on sideways thus using more of the length of the form. Thought must be given, when planning the apparatus and setting the task, as the ease or difficulty in the use of directions often varies with the situation.

Whatever task is set, the use of all the directions may be explored and established, gradually being deepened and so helping the girls to manipulate themselves in the space around them.

4. Levels of Space

By levels in Space is meant areas, zones or regions of space in terms of high, medium and low strata in relationship to the body when standing. The legs move naturally in the low level, the torso in the medium level and the shoulders upwards in the high level. Thus when moving close to the floor as when rolling or walking on hands and feet, the whole body moves in the low level : similarly when jumping or rising away from the floor more of the body moves in the high area. The levels, or space strata, remain constant, but it is possible to move the different parts of the body in the less natural areas, and this leads to agility ;   for example, the hands may move into the low level and the feet into the high level. The whole body should move in the different levels for if only the low level is used the movement becomes "earthbound" ; use of the medium level helps to get the body further from the floor whilst the high level often involves elevation. This awareness of the use of the different levels helps to give variety in movement, involving the use of different parts of the body to support the weight and a realisation of where one is, even if inverted, in the Personal Space.

When changing from one level to another it is the upward and downward directions which will be used ; thus when moving in the low area, an upward direction will take the body first into the medium zone and, if continued, into the high level.

5. Central and peripheral use of Space

The awareness of Directions and Levels in the Personal

Space is essential and must be used from the beginnings of the teaching of movement, but there are certain aspects of the study of Space which may be used with more advanced classes which will widen and deepen the understanding of where they can move : the following aspects mentioned in this chapter come into this category.

Central and Peripheral pathways through space can perhaps best be described if likened to a wheel ; Central movement uses the pathways occupied by the spokes of the wheel which run towards and away from the centre, whilst Peripheral movement travels round the rim or circumference of the wheel. The wheel can be placed at any angle or level, its hub being relative to the centre of the body. Thus movement can take place in a variety of levels and directions, but always having a relationship to its centre. As there are different sized wheels so the extension into the space may be varied at will (see Extension).

Central movement is very linked with the fundamental body actions of Bending and Stretching, when the movement starts in the centre of the body and spreads along a straight pathway to the extremities and returns back to the centre — the movement flowing in and out, to and from the centre. The stress now is not on the body as in Bending and Stretching, but on the pathway through which the body passes or travels. The accent may be placed on either the inward or the outward movement, being taken with varying tensions and speeds in the various Levels, Directions and Extensions in Space.

Peripheral movement may be linked with Twisting of the body which is necessary in order that the chosen part of the body, the foot, knee, seat or hand, can move round the centre in a curved pathway, whatever the level or direction. Opportunity should be given to explore these pathways with different parts of the body with a continual change of the supporting base. The radius of the arc through which the body travels will vary according to the extension of the body, thus influencing the size of the peripheral pathway. If the feet move peripherally, the weight being taken on the hands, more space will be used than if it is the seat (the legs being bent) or the fist, if on the feet, will make a larger arc than if supported on the seat.

Opportunity and guidance should be given to girls to explore the possibilities of taking the weight on a variety of parts of the body whilst moving through the space using both central or peripheral pathways. It will be found that in transferring the weight from one part of the body to another, either pathway may be used, such an example is when transferring the weight from the feet onto the hands : if done with a stress on central movement the weight is taken on the hands with the legs bent and then stretched : if the stress is on a peripheral pathway the legs swing upwards through a curved pathway until over the hands. The starting and ending positions are similar, but since it is the pathways through the space with which we are concerned, the way of getting there is important.

Sequences of movement may be made stressing the contrast in the two pathways through the space leading logically from one to the other through transference of weight and varied Effort content giving resilience of movement. These aspects may be used as Movement Tasks with apparatus, but it must be remembered that most sequences (vaults) will involve both pathways to some degree, though the one or the other may be accented and developed within the vault.

6. *Extension in space*

This aspect is involved with how much space is used, how far the movement extends into the Personal Space. A small amount of space may be used and by stretching out the body a greater amount is used until at its greatest stretch it extends to its fullest in the space. The extremes of this awareness of the use of space, as well as the degrees in between, are important for full exploitation of the medium in which we move. So often girls are to be seen moving in a limited sphere being unaware of its fullest extent. Skill and confidence to use this full extension should be given, as it is often the insecure, self-conscious girl who uses little space, whilst the selection of the degrees in between the extremes, suitable for the task in hand, calls for muscular control and judgement.

When making classes aware of extension into space, the extremes may be contrasted at first, later the growth or decrease in its use, thus a similar pathway may be used with the gradual increase or decrease in extension. When stepping, small steps may be contrasted with large ; or a space rhythm may be developed such as small, medium, large steps, the latter requiring a greater awareness of the space achieved through greater muscular control. Although the stress has been on the use of the space, in order to achieve this Effort has been involved, particularly the Weight Factor, for the further into the space the body is moved the greater the tension needed to move it. Variation in the speed of each phrase (Time Factor) will further develop the Effort content, and finally, directions will add further to the interest and skill of a sequence, again showing the absolute integration in the use of the Body, Effort and Space.

This awareness of Space may be used in conjunction with many other aspects of movement as in Bending and Stretching, Twisting, the Meeting and Parting of selected parts, the Importance of a part, with other Space aspects such as Central and Peripheral movement, the use of Directions or within the Planes of movement, thus bringing to the consciousness of the performer the awareness of how much space she is using through its contrasts and rhythms.

7. *The planes of movement*

The planes of movement are directly connected with the three dimensions, each dimension being flattened out, as it were, to give a surface : thus the up and down dimension has a certain width, but the stress is on the height and depth.

When in relation to the body the plane divides it into a front and back, this is known as the **Frontal or Door plane.** The relative orientation of this plane to the human body may be felt by standing with the feet apart and both arms stretched obliquely upwards and sideways when the four extremities give the four corners of the plane.

The side to side dimension gives rise to the **Transverse or Table plane,** the stress being from side to side with a certain forward and backwardness, dividing the body into upper and lower halves and running parallel to the floor as though the body were surrounded by a table. The orientation may be indicated by standing on one leg and bending forward to a right angle at the hips stretching both arms obliquely forwards and sideways with the free leg obliquely backwards and sideways. The three extremities indicate three of the corners of the plane.

The forwards and backwards dimension gives rise to the **Sagittal or Wheel plane,** the stress being forwards and backwards with a certain height and depth dividing the body into right and left sides. The points of orientation may be indicated by raising one arm and leg obliquely forwards and upwards and the other arm obliquely backwards and upwards.

Movement in each plane has certain characteristics, that in the *Door plane* stressing up and down movement leads to *elevation*, the *Table plane* encircling the body leads to twisting and *turning* and the *Wheel* plane as its name implies to *locomotion*, particularly in the forwards and backwards direction. All movement, since the body is three dimensional, involves all these planes, but many body actions fall mainly into a certain plane. Bending sideways and stretching to the upright; the transference of weight from the right hand to the left, onto the left foot, then the right in a sideways direction, are mainly in the Door plane. Thus stress on moving in a certain plane will lead to certain ways of moving and help to clarify where in the space movement takes place.

In the gymnastics lesson the main characteristics of these

can therefore be taught in that way. These being definite actions, they are more likely to lead to movement than the making of shapes, and should be continually in mind whenever this approach is used as a theme.

After exploration of each of these shapes with the use of weight transference and different directions, levels and Effort content, sequences may be made on the floor. It is advisable to limit the class by setting a definite task, as all the fundamental actions are involved, otherwise any sequence of movement would fulfil the task. Similarly when using the apparatus, tasks set might be, at the box "Move in a rounded way", at the Window-ladder "Move in a twisted way" or at the horse "Move stressing the length of the body".

CHAPTER XII

Apparatus Work

THE work on the apparatus should take up about half of the lesson time and is the climax to the lesson, so naturally we ask, "What is its value?"

It should be the culmination of all the work done previously on the floor ; whether alone, in two's, small groups or using small apparatus. It provides opportunity for the younger girls to use their natural instincts to jump, climb and swing, which, due to the town life and the tendency of the present day to watch rather than do oneself, they are denied. For the older girls, if well trained, there is opportunity to maintain this agility acquired in youth, the apparatus providing more difficult situations, and they obtain both mental and physical satisfaction from solving the problems set. At whatever age, being faced with a problem makes the girls get to grips with it and encourages such characteristics as grit and determination. The nature of the task set on apparatus sets certain limitations and yet allows for individual interpretation, thus encouraging invention and initiative. So long as the set task is fulfilled, the girls are able to carry it out in various ways according to their natural movement abilities, thus the less able girl is not made to feel inferior ; for example, if using the box where the task is to "Get on and off with different parts of the body taking the weight on the apparatus" — the agile girl may land on the box with her feet, whilst the less agile, being heavier or having less spring, may land on the box with her "middle or seat". Both have fulfilled the task, but the former may be impossible for the less able girl at first. May it be pointed out that the teacher should always try to extend the girls — helping them to achieve more and more, judging when she needs to encourage and praise and when to press them to greater effort.

The variety of widths and heights of apparatus demands judgement, daring and attack and needs to be made gradually more difficult, alternating exploration with repetition ; even the least daring girl gains more confidence. The teacher should be aware of the more frightened individuals and provide for their needs, by having similar apparatus, but of an easier height or width giving them the opportunity to choose which apparatus they go and work on. For example, if the forms are being used inclined into the ribstalls, the lower one might be in number six whilst the highest one was in number ten. The task set is the same at both and as the girls become more proficient they may move to the higher piece or where possible be allowed to raise the apparatus — thus whatever stage they are at there is incentive and opportunity to progress.

All movement on apparatus should be purposeful. During the period of exploration the girls should find out, with the guidance of the teacher when necessary, what is profitable ; they need to select, rejecting unsuitable ideas in movement, before deciding on the finished sequence : thus they learn to discriminate and discipline themselves. They should then work on the vault until they are able to do it well, so learning persistence and what is considered a good standard of movement. Few girls can do this alone, and much depends upon the understanding of movement and the standards of the teacher, together with her contact and understanding of all of her class.

The work on the apparatus is often referred to as **vaulting** and the sequence of movement using the apparatus as a **vault.** This sequence of movement on apparatus, or vault, consists of the **Approach, Contact** with the apparatus and the **Recovery.** Each part is of equal importance to the whole. The Approach should not be ignored for it is essential as the preparation for what is to follow on the apparatus. Similarly, the Recovery or landing, as it follows inevitably after what has happened on the apparatus.

Preparation Approach	Action Contact with the apparatus	Recovery Landing

In planning work to be covered the teacher needs to be aware of this, so that she can train the girls first on the floor then using easy low apparatus, such as forms or mats, before presenting them with the larger apparatus such as a horse or bars.

1. *The preparation or approach*

Before starting to move the vaulter needs to put her mind to the task in hand ; to **concentrate** and be alert and to know, at least, how she will start ; whether she knows exactly every detail that follows will depend upon the stage her vault has reached. She may be exploring and so not quite sure of where or how the flow of movement will take her ; or she may be working on final details of a skilful performance ; but whatever it is, full concentration and anticipation are necessary. The vaulter usually starts from a stationary position and approaches the apparatus on her feet preparatory to the "take-off" from the floor. What action is to follow will affect this approach ; for example, if the vaulter is landing on the apparatus with her feet there needs to be a great crescendo in **speed** and **tension** reaching the maximum at the sudden "take-off" from the floor, so that the body is lifted into the air to land on top of the apparatus. This gradual crescendo of the run needs practice and can be taught earlier in the lesson and then applied to work with the apparatus. The **length** of the run before reaching the climax can be decreased gradually and the shorter this is the more suitable when in conjunction with apparatus. On the other hand, in contrast to the above, the vaulter may be leaving the floor from her hands with the "seat" coming onto the apparatus, in this case a slower approach is needed with the continuous transference of weight from the walking feet onto the hands which then push strongly off the floor, causing the "seat" to arrive on the apparatus. Again work can be done on the floor or using low apparatus involving the change of body weight and the increase of tension in the arms.

Often girls are allowed to amble up to the apparatus and then scramble onto it due to this vital beginning of the vault being forgotten — they have fulfilled the task of "Getting onto the apparatus" — but good movement is our aim.

Besides the speed and length of approach to the apparatus the **angle** needs to be considered ; is it from the end, the side or obliquely ? All these may be experienced in simple ways before using more difficult pieces of apparatus.

Thus it can be seen that the **length** of approach, the **speed**, the **tension** and the **angle**, together with the part of the body "**taking off**" from, are all important in this stage of the vault.

2. *Contact with the apparatus*

Suggestions have been made concerning the "Approach" and it is suggested that the "Recovery" of a vault should be considered *before* the more difficult tasks which are concerned with "Contact" with the apparatus, are attempted, as it is essential to recover from any vault safely, however simple.

Before any tasks are set the girls need to become familiar with the characteristics of the various apparatus available, exploring the nature of the obstacles. There are certain factors which have to be considered : whether the apparatus is **stable** or **mobile,** some pieces of apparatus are firm and solid, such as the bars and the box, which give firm support ; others move and therefore are more difficult to work with providing a mobile base, and the more the apparatus moves the more difficult the adjustment of the body on it, as with ropes, rope ladders or trapeze.

The **height** of the apparatus is a difficulty to some girls whereas others do not mind, and this, apart from the actual task set, may present a problem to individuals. The **width** of the apparatus may make the task easier or more difficult ; for it is easier to land onto a wide box than onto the narrow bar of the same height ; but if the task were to get over the apparatus, it might be found easier to get over the narrow bar rather than the wide box. If it is a case of travelling along apparatus the wider it is the easier it is, as the adjustment of the body weight is easier on a wide surface.

Experience should be given in using all types of apparatus and the length of time given to this will vary according to the previous experience and natural ability of the class. This exploration of the apparatus is necessary, even with the most advanced classes, when presented with a new arrangement or combination, but here the length of time may only be that of two or three turns.

The introduction of **ACTION TASKS** may then follow. By these are meant problems dealing with the apparatus itself. Such tasks which may be set include "Get on and off" (such apparatus as forms and horses), "Go along" (bars or horse), "Go up and down" (ropes or window ladder), "Get over" (box or bar), "Go through", "In and out" or "Round", according to the shape and nature of the apparatus. Single actions may be set or suitable combinations.

This is a good stage to teach several fundamentals in relationship to all vaulting. First, when a task has been set, the teacher should be sure it is understood and then insist on it being *carried out*. Help can be given in exploring the task in conjunction with the different approaches and their effort on the main action, but the second important fundamental is the idea of a vault being a *sequence* of movement, and this should be made clear and become habitual to the girls.

After a period of exploration, the teacher having guided the class where necessary, the skill of moving matters, and has to be coached, giving the girls an appreciation of a standard of work. This is achieved through each girl selecting one idea from her many ways of fulfilling the task set, and working on it for some time. There is great satisfaction gained in discovering new vaults, but also in the repetition of a skill done to the peak of one's ability, and it is here that real bodily skill, judgement and confidence are developed, besides standards and judgement of good movement.

It is not necessary to experience all the possible Action Tasks before developing vaults through the use of **MOVEMENT TASKS**. When using an Action Task it was the apparatus that set the problem, but with a Movement Task it is the movement situation which disciplines the result. The Movement task on the apparatus often links with the movement content of the first part of the lesson and should be thought of in conjunction with it. It is possible to set an Action task in conjunction with a Movement task or only a Movement task, leaving the use of the apparatus free. Whichever is done, all that has been learnt previously concerning the Approach and Recovery and the sequence as a whole should be maintained. If working on "Awareness of different parts of the body" the girls might be set a task such as "Get on and off (Action) the apparatus using different parts of the body (Movement)". Time should be given for the girls to **explore** the possibilities of the task, the teacher helping by suggestion and demonstration of girls' ideas, which will help to widen the vocabulary of the class and give confidence to explore further ; followed by **selection** and **repetition** to make the vault as skilled as possible. In this task the girls should be encouraged to choose a different part at each piece of apparatus or else it may be found that the same part of the body has been used at every piece. This is an instance where the observation of the teacher and her knowledge of the movement of the individuals in her class are so essential, in order to ensure an all round development of the girls. Some of the more profitable parts of the body to take weight on the apparatus are "middles", "seats", knee or knees and foot or feet, with their appropriate "Approaches" and "Recoveries". In these examples, and in fact in all vaulting, unless otherwise stated, it is assumed that the hands, in addition, may be used.

Other suggestions of Tasks might be "To curl (Movement) at some point"; "To stretch (Movement)"; "To twist (Movement)"; "Roll (Movement) along (Action) the apparatus"; "Get on (Action) symmetrically (Movement) and come off (Action) asymmetrically (Movement)"; "Fly (Movement) over (Action) the apparatus" and so on. All of the above Movement tasks are concerned with the body, but aspects of Space may similarly be used, such as the use of directions, when the task might be "Get on (Action) sideways (Movement) and come off (Action)"; "Get on and come off with a turn". The Space aspect of Near and Far, taking the relationship of the vaulter to the apparatus, may be used as in "Get over as near to (far away from) the apparatus as possible" or "Get over (Action) with the feet (Body, Movement) as far away (Space, Movement) as possible." In the latter example there is one Action task and two Movement tasks, one concerned with the body and one the space. Other more advanced Space tasks could include Central and Peripheral ways of moving or limitations within a definite plane of movement (see chapter on Space).

So far nothing has been mentioned about the Effort content in vaulting, but it is such an integral part of movement that it is always there, and cannot be isolated as some of the Body and Space aspects of movement may be, and should be considered and worked on in every vault. Its importance has been stressed in conjunction with the fundamental body actions which will have been taught on the floor and it must be maintained when using the apparatus. The Effort changes should be stressed as a rhythm of the whole sequence, with the crescendos, diminuendos and climaxes which lead to ease and variety in the vault. Careful thought is necessary before an aspect of Effort content is set as a Movement task, or else it may be very artificial as in such a case as "Get onto the box as strongly as possible" — this is absurd! In order to lift the body onto the box, a certain tension is essential, too much

would take the vaulter too far, too little would be insufficient
to achieve the task. Teaching the use of the Weight Factor
in relationship to apparatus is the skill in judging the tensions
required to fulfil the task skilfully. Thus the setting out of
apparatus of different heights and widths in contrast to each
other and consciously being aware of the different tensions
required, gives opportunity to train its awareness (see chapter
on Weight Factor).

Similarly, with the Time Factor care needs to be taken,
for changes within the vault may make it skilful or dangerous
— just the right increase or decrease of speed with the smooth
transition from one to the other leads to skill, whereas the
whole done at a fast speed has no rhythm or skill. The teacher
needs to observe well in order to help the girls, and get them
to help each other, to find where it would help the vaulter
to speed up or slow down, thus gaining the feeling for the
rhythm which is right for that vault. It is possible to set a
Movement task involving the Time Factor such as "Go along
with part of the vault done very slowly (quickly)". This helps
to make the girls aware of the change of speed and gives them
freedom of choice at which point to move slowly (quickly),
though once they have the feeling for resilient movement it
is the natural rhythm one would deepen (see chapter on Time
Factor).

Thus the Weight and Time Factors are integral parts of the
rhythm of a vault, they must be present in order to achieve
any action and should be coached as such, though it is possible
to a certain degree to set profitable tasks which will emphasise
the Effort content, such as "Initiating movement with part of
the body", or if the same phrase is repeated several times as
in such a task as "Over and under a bar continuously". Such
questions as "Where is the accent ?", "Where is more tension
needed ?", "Where is the movement quicker or slower ?"
may help the vaulter become aware of the Effort changes.

The Flow Factor in the sense of continuity of movement,
as against a pausing or holding, may be coached ; thus the

whole vault may be continuous or there may be a moment
of holding or stillness, where the flow of the movement is
arrested at some suitable point within the sequence.

3. *The recovery or landing*

If girls get onto apparatus, of necessity, they must be able
to get off with safety. This involves a variety of ways and
therefore these need training, so perhaps they should be
considered before much stress is put onto the middle part
of the vault. Often the girls are left to flop or scramble off
as best they can and the skill of the vault as a whole is lost —
it should be a recovery from what has happened before,
bringing it to a satisfactory ending. The two usual parts of
the body meeting the floor after a vault are the feet and the
hands.

If landing **on the feet** it may be onto one or both of them,
according to the height of the apparatus and nature of the
vault, but in either case the legs must be prepared to take
the weight of the body and so need enough tension in them,
to receive it and lower it gently to the ground, and at the
same time to reduce the speed of the moving body. Too much
tension leads to jarring, too little into a collapse in a heap
on the floor (see chapters on the Effort content in Transference of Weight). The meeting of the floor may be done
in a balanced way where the body weight falls vertically over
the feet (see On- and Off-balance) with a resilient recoil up
to standing ; or it may be more off-balance where the body
weight is moved smoothly from one part to another along
the ground whether remaining on the feet, which are used
alternately, or using other parts of the body in succession,
until the momentum has died down and stillness is achieved.

If landing **with the hands** meeting the ground first, it is
the arms which take the weight of the body and after that
the vaulter may go into a curled roll in any direction or bring
the feet down in various directions, the body being curled
or stretched out. This bearing of the body weight on the

arms, if only momentarily, needs strength of arm, also the ability to transfer the weight smoothly from them to other parts of the body, and considerable exploration of the possible ways, and practice at floor level, should be given before attempting it from the higher apparatus.

Rarely is it safe for other parts of the body to contact the floor first, though if the apparatus is just the right height it is possible for the shoulders to do so, followed by a rolling recovery.

There are a great variety of ways of meeting the floor with the feet and the hands, and time should be given to explore the possibilities, with guidance from the teacher; then repetition until the girls become skilled. Points to remember are the adjustment of the weight to give a balanced or an off-balanced meeting of the floor; a curling or stretching of the body; the various combinations of the use of the feet and hands and whether followed by other parts of the body coming in contact with the floor, with the use of various directions, tensions and speeds of movement.

Some possible ways of using the apparatus

The apparatus may be **used once** with a simple vault of Approach — Action — Recovery, using Action and Movement tasks appropriate to the stage and ability of the class.

It is also possible to use the single piece of apparatus **twice** or more times — the Recovery then becomes the Preparation for the second Action :

$$\left\| \text{ Approach } - \text{ Action } \left\{ \begin{matrix} \text{Recovery} \\ \text{Preparation} \end{matrix} \right\} - \text{ Action } - \text{ Recovery } \right\|$$

This requires good resilience or skill in the interplay of the Weight and Time Factors, fine adjustment of the body weight with judgement and anticipation. The longer sequence gives greater opportunity to vary the possibilities of Weight and

Time changes as well as the various Space and Body aspects possible, but each vault, however short or long, needs to have its climax.

Another way to lengthen and make the vault more difficult is to use **more than one piece** of apparatus placing the two or more pieces close to each other using varying heights and widths, or combining the use of a more stable type with a mobile type.

As it was possible to work **with a partner** or in small groups on the floor, similarly it is on apparatus. A simple beginning might be such a task as "Go along the apparatus and pass each other on the way", or in two's girls might shadow or mirror each other. A more advanced task would be where they take each other's weight ; when one could help the other to balance in stillness at some point, or actively help to lift her. More difficult still might be where the weight of one girl is counterbalanced against the weight of the other — should one of the pair fail, they will both fall. This is skilled and needs much practice on the floor first ; reliability is essential and sensitivity between the girls necessary. They might work together, with the stress on the interplay of the timing of one girl's actions with the other. If one girl is a fraction of a second late in moving it may mean a collision. Their movements have to be adapted to each other so that at one moment one girl may have to move quickly whilst the other moves more slowly, thus they become masters of intertiming and speed of moving.

Similar tasks may be done in **three's,** but when three minds have to work together it is even more difficult than two.

Small groups of three or four girls can work with each other, with simple known Action or Movement tasks, where they make a rhythmic sequence. Variations in relationship can be used where they all move together, or two and two, or one after the other soon sets the class to work busily. Such a task might follow after having worked on the Action or Movement task individually, now their chief concern will be the new and additional task concerned with relationships.

At whatever stage the class is there should be time for **Exploration** within the limits of the task, being *guided* by the teacher to new discoveries, always aware of the influence and possibilities of the Approach and Recovery ; then time to **Develop** and deepen a selected vault, where the content in relation to the Body, Effort, Space and Relationships is worked on for sufficient time to give the vaulter satisfaction which leads to a **skilled** performance. What has been learnt in the early stages should be used in all later ones, so that there is a gradual increase in repertoire and skill.

ORGANISATION OF THE APPARATUS

It is usual to work on apparatus in small groups giving opportunity to have as many turns as possible. The number in each group ideally should not be more than three or four girls, so that one is vaulting, one returning from her vault, one watching to criticise helpfully and one preparing herself for her turn — thus all are actively occupied mentally or physically or both.

It is much easier for the teacher to help girls who are new to apparatus, if all the groups use the same apparatus. It is more difficult when the groups use different apparatus, even with the same task, and the most difficult when each group has a different task using different apparatus. After the initial stages the second of these suggestions is the most usual where the task is the same for all, but the groups use different apparatus.

First the teacher needs to decide **what task** she feels suitable for the class, and then to select **suitable apparatus.** If there are about thirty girls in the class there will have to be at least eight groups, and although it has been said above that it is easier to have eight similar pieces of apparatus, this is not possible for long, due to limited apparatus. It may be possible to have four groups working on one type of apparatus and four groups on another type; or two groups on similar apparatus repeated four times, or eight different pieces may be used, with the same task. However, to get round to each of the eight sections, have time to explore and then work on a vault, would take many lessons, so this needs to be taken into consideration when planning the apparatus and it is suggested that four different pieces are used which are duplicated.

Thought then needs to be given to the actual **placing** of the apparatus in the gymnasium. When approaching the apparatus the girls should not cross the approach of other girls at other pieces of apparatus, and therefore allowance must be made in all directions round the apparatus. Some of the older gymnasia have low ceilings or overhead structures and then care is needed in the placing of the high apparatus in order to avoid them. Windows through which the sun shines may cause difficulty in seeing and the approach should be away from this bright light rather than into it. The type of movement expected also must be considered; thus the apparatus which demands suspension from the arms should alternate with that which uses other parts of the body.

Thought needs to be given to the order and method of **changing round** from one section to another, so that it can take place in an orderly and logical manner without causing uncertainty as to where to go, argument or dissatisfaction. A circular tour, whether of all eight sections or of the four in either half of the gymnasium is usually possible to arrange. With all this to bear in mind, a diagram showing the placing of the apparatus and direction of changing round is often helpful to the teacher, as part of her lesson preparation.

HANDLING AND CARE OF THE APPARATUS

Care should be taken in moving the apparatus for two reasons, primarily to prevent immediate injury to the girls and secondly damage to the apparatus, which if strained may

Fig. 13. Moving in the
Wheel plane.

(*Face page* 90)

Fig. 14. Moving in the
Table plane.

Fig. 15. Coming off the apparatus foward onto the hands.

Fig. 16. Coming off the apparatus backwards onto the hands.

Fig. 17. Coming off the apparatus sideways onto the hands with the legs straight.

lead to accidents in the future. When the apparatus is moved it should be done quickly but without undue haste, and placed quietly into position ; continued rough treatment leads to such things as ill-fitting bars and layers of boxes. All apparatus should be lifted and not dragged along the floor and two or more girls are needed, evenly placed, so that they share the weight equally between them. To lift any weight, at any time, the knees should be bent and then straightened, the strain being taken by the strong muscles of the thighs, and not by the weaker ones of the back. Girls need to be taught this, for few do it instinctively, the more usual way is to lift with the legs straight, all the weight being taken by the back, which may lead to a strain.

The girls should be made responsible for their apparatus, making sure that pegs are in the uprights at the bars ; that the pommels and legs of the horse are firm and of the same height ; that mats are flat and where needed ; but the final responsibility lies with the teacher who should always check them. The way classes handle their apparatus is indicative of the training they have received in self-discipline, responsibility and reliability, and time taken to ensure this is by no means wasted and is also essential from the safety point of view.

CHAPTER XIII

Working with other People

GIRLS enjoy working together whatever their age ; it is of value to them both from the movement point of view, and in the development of character and personality. Young senior girls learn to co-operate and to understand the simpler aspects of movement involved ; the middle age range may need the help and moral support of ·a partner, thus helping to get rid of self-consciousness and helping them to regain confidence through their interest in other people ; whilst the older seniors gain from skilful co-operation of working together in fulfilling more difficult tasks.

Working together may be in two's, three's or four's where every girl is *essential to the whole*. If the numbers are larger it is very difficult to get everyone fully participating the whole time, and it deteriorates into having turns one after the other : working together means doing things which could not be done in quite the same way or would be impossible to do alone. It is therefore a task of relationships in addition to the movement task involved — both need to be clear and definite.

1. *Working together without physical contact*

Under this heading may be included the relationship with another person in that one is willing to help the other by giving **constructive criticism;** the girls learn to be more tolerant towards each other, willing to accept advice and learn to give it constructively. In some cases individuals may need help in working together in this way. This way of working together, taking a certain responsibility for each other's movement after they have had opportunity to work on it individually, is useful at any stage and at all ages. Through having to help a partner, the understanding of what is involved is deepened ; through observing movement a feeling for, and judgement of, good and poor movement is developed, and the one moving improves as a result of the individual help given, particularly if the teacher is helpful in her guidance of what the observer is to coach.

After working on a sequence of movement on the floor alone, the girls may take a partner and one of them **teach her partner her sequence.** This makes her clarify her own movement and know what is involved. The same values, as above, will be involved, but in addition the "learner" has to discipline herself to someone else's movement in the way she uses her Body, the Effort rhythm and in the use of the Space. This is of value as some girls tend to develop a "favourite side" or way of moving rhythmically and in this way their skill and vocabulary will be enlarged and their concentration and movement memory deepened.

A task such as **"Working together to make a sequence"**, being set some definite movement task may be given. Here co-operation right from the start is needed and the vocabulary of one or both girls may be widened due to the pooling of movement ideas. If one is a very able girl and one less able, there will be the need for adaptation ; the able girl will need to be tolerant towards her partner and give way to a certain extent and be willing to help her, whilst the less able girl will probably be extended that little bit further than if working alone, and so gain a little more physical skill as well as confidence. There is value to both partners, but in different ways.

Another way of working together involving more agility is to **use a partner as an obstacle** to go over and under her. These actions may be used separately or in conjunction with each other, but the girls alternately take it in turns to be the obstacle and the mover, the change over from one to the other following on logically and continuously. It is the "obstacle" who really sets the situation by the shape and height of her body, whether to be gone over or under. The "mover" has to adapt to the situation calling for constructive and quick thinking for both partners.

2. Working together with physical contact but no weight bearing

An example of this way of working is when two girls hold one or two hands, with such a task as "Twisting with a partner". They take it in turns to be the one twisting and the one helping. Often new situations arise, due to the unusual contact, which have to be dealt with and the movement imagination and vocabulary are developed out of sheer necessity in the first stages of exploration. The assisting partner must be ready to help and guide her partner, whether she be meeting the floor or getting away from it, whether she be leading the twist with the upper or lower half of the body, and the greater her anticipation the more sensitive should she become to her partner's movement. The twisting of her partner will in all probability cause the support herself to twist and then she should follow the logical pathway of movement in order to untwist herself.

3. Working together involving various degrees of weight bearing

Here one girl supports the weight of her partner. Among other things the strength of the one bearing the weight is increased, but it is advisable for girls of similar size and weight to work together.

One way is where the partner is **used momentarily**, rather as a piece of apparatus to push off from; the support should remain static, but needs to be firm and reliable, giving resistance to the momentary thrust of her partner.

It is possible **to take a partner's weight completely** as in such a task as "Balance in stillness on your partner". Exploration of the various parts of the body in contact with each other is necessary and the smaller the area the greater the skill needed as the task is one of weight adjustment and Flow. The girls can take it in turns to balance and support forming a logical continuous sequence which calls for co-operation, adaptation and accurate weight adjustment as well as trust in and reliability of one another's support. The difficulty in making the sequence logical and continuous is very bound up with the fact that the end of the first idea has to be the beginning of the second. Therefore it is no good choosing three or four ideas and trying to put them together. It is better to start with one idea and *then select* what will easily follow on after the first.

In the above examples the support has been stationary whilst taking her partner's weight, but it is possible for her to be moving and **actively lifting her partner** which involves the additional complication of timing, and strength not only to support but to lift her partner. In such a task as "Helping a partner to get high", the one going high should propel herself as high as she can and then the partner, just at the right moment, adds her strength in the same direction to send her even further, thus giving the partner a greater experience of height. To achieve this the support needs to time the push accurately and to place herself as far as is possible under her partner in order to lift her. When taking this alternately as in a sequence, quick thought, adjustment one to the other, co-operation and skill are essential. Time should be given to explore suitable grasps ; various ways of transferring the weight and parts of the body involved, which will lead to a variety of relationships ; the degrees of tension needed and the timing ; before there is selection and a sequence evolved. When the sequence has been formed it should be worked on until a standard of skill is achieved forming a rhythmic whole and giving satisfaction to the performers.

In a similar way such a task may be carried out in three's, the experience of the one "going high" should be even greater and can very profitably be used to give deeper movement experiences as in the example above or in such tasks as "Flight" which may be taken in any direction. The fact that three girls are working together instead of two makes co-operation more difficult and therefore greater awareness of each other is demanded.

More advanced ways of working together in two's or three's may involve an **interplay of the body weight** of one person with that of another, where the one counterbalances the other ; it can be an even balancing or the one may "tip the balance" and the one partner has to exert force with a gradual release or crescendo until the other has achieved stability. Without the counterweight and strength of the one partner the other would fall. This involves skilful body weight adjustment and interplay of tensions with absolute trust in one's partner which calls for complete reliability ; as the latter increases so does the confidence which allows the movement to go further. Any lack of concentration or unreliability in any way will lead to falling.

Another way of working together in two's or three's might be referred to as the **"Intertiming of movements"** where split second timing is of utmost importance. If the first person does not get out of the way or into the right place just at the right moment, the second (and third) will not be able to move as planned — this involves complete mastery of one's own body and the varying speeds at which one is moving in relation to the other(s), as her (their) safety may depend upon it.

The above suggestions have not been related to apparatus but it is possible when the girls are able and reliable in working together on the floor to work in similar ways on the apparatus, but it should be remembered that the height and the smaller surface area of the apparatus presents greater difficulty than when moving on the floor. Some ways are more difficult and require more training both physically and in reliable co-operation with each other. The standard and previous experience of the girls should be an indication to the teacher as to which way she chooses to set a task, rather than the age of the girls. Older less able girls will benefit from and enjoy working in two's copying each other, using such apparatus as the window-ladder, double bars, horse or box, as would a class of twelve-year-olds. In a similar way a group rhythm may be worked on, using the action task of "On and off the apparatus", with apparatus at a suitable height according to the ability of the class, whether twelve- or sixteen-year-olds. As individuals they will be familiar with the many ways of getting on and off the apparatus, but now they have to co-operate with two or three other people. The different possible relationships will need exploring, such as all arriving on the apparatus together, in canon, two and two or two and one, according to the number in the group. A decision has to be made whether all in the group use the same way of getting on and off, or whether each individual fulfils the task in her own way. The relationship combined with the use of the Body and the Effort content of their actions should form a whole rhythmic sequence of movement, every girl being essential to the whole.

In all cases it is necessary to guide or limit the girls by setting a task — just to say "work together" is *not* sufficient. There is no fast rule, but some quite definite task of relationships together with a movement or action task is necessary, for example, "Work together actively helping partner (Relationships) to go high (movement)". Whether the work is on the floor or on apparatus, the tasks need exploring as to the possible relationships and to the movement possibilities : then selection made from these ideas to build a logical sequence, which may then be worked on until skill and satisfaction is gained. All this takes considerable time, and when using apparatus the teacher must ensure that there is plenty of apparatus available, ideally one piece for each pair or group.

Thus it can be seen that in working together opportunity is given to experience and increase movement skill in actions

Fig. 20. Working with others — lifting in threes.

Fig. 21. Working with others — initiating in threes.

Fig. 22. Working with others on the apparatus — copying a partner.

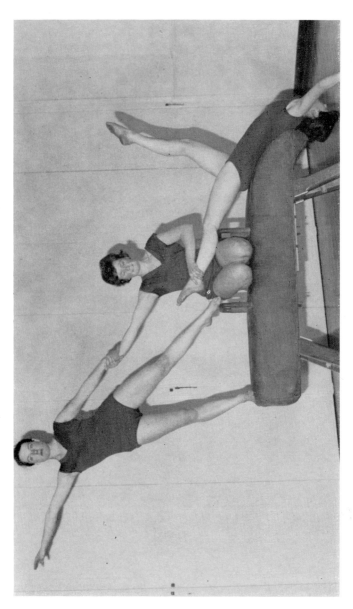

Fig. 23. Working with others on the apparatus — assisting in threes.

CHAPTER XIV

The Lesson

THE amount of time for each lesson varies very much from one school to another, being as short as thirty-five minutes in some, to as long as one hour and fifteen minutes in others. Time has to be deducted for changing at the beginning and showering at the end, which in the shorter lesson mentioned gives less than half an hour of teaching time. Whatever the length of time available half of it should be spent learning to move on the floor and the other half using apparatus. If large quantities of apparatus are used considerable time can be spent getting it out, leaving relatively little time to use it ; so training in the handling of apparatus is a necessity in order to allow time for its use, as well as that of teaching girls how to lift, carry and manipulate heavy objects in conjunction with each other.

1. *The form of a gymnastic lesson*

It is important to develop an attitude of work from the moment the girls enter the gymnasium. There are many possible ways, but whichever is chosen the girls should start to work on the floor as soon as they enter the gymnasium, moving all parts of their bodies, freeing their joints from any stiffness by bending, stretching and twisting and gaining mastery over themselves by transferring their weight with the use of varied tensions and speeds. They might practise freely some of the work of the previous lesson, or some aspect of work in which the individual knows she needs practice, or the teacher might set them a simple task such as "Get warm by transferring your weight" or "Twisting".

The first part of the lesson or **Introduction** is where the lesson theme is introduced and the teaching begins. It should be lively and active, usually concerned with some form of locomotion, to give a change from sitting in desks, and satisfying the needs of all young people to move vigorously. It should get the class into the right mood for the main part of the lesson to follow, using some of the energy of the energetic or stimulating the lethargic into a more active lively response.

The movement content of the activity should be within the ability of the class, though the situation in which it is presented may be new to them ; thus there is concentration needed but not of great depth ; it is a time to introduce or remind the class of the aspect of movement with which the lesson is concerned.

The interest of the class should be gained and the mind and body enlivened in preparation for the more difficult work to follow.

The first part of the lesson has a stress on locomotion which usually involves considerable work for the legs, so the stress of the second part of the lesson or **Development** of the theme has a stress on the use of the spine, involving the whole body and the movement may take place more in an area rather than using the whole floor space. The power of concentration has built up to its peak and the body is at its best physiologically, so it is here that new aspects of work are developed or familiar ones further explored and deepened.

The Introduction and Development of the theme on the floor should together take half the lesson and in the second half apparatus should be used. If the lesson is reasonably long it is very useful to have a **Class Activity,** where the whole class work on similar apparatus such as mats, forms or bars. This serves as a link and a preparation for work on the larger apparatus and gives the teacher greater opportunity to help the whole class, as all the apparatus used is the same. This is a good time to teach any necessary basic skill. It may have been observed, for example, that during the apparatus work many girls, when using high bars or ropes, hung on them in a sack-like way ; therefore instead of helping each one individually as she came to the apparatus the teacher can teach good hanging to the whole class. Various ways of meeting the floor whether with hands or feet may be taught using forms, before attempting similar landings from the higher apparatus, is just another example.

When introducing new apparatus to a class, whether it be mats, forms, ropes or bars, it is much easier for the teacher to ensure that the method of getting out and carrying is understood, if only dealing with the one type of apparatus at once. At first it might be found useful to have two or even three Class Activities following each other in the one lesson, taking the place completely of the group apparatus work.

Besides the above, this part of the lesson may be used for working with other people, whether in two's or three's. There can be great educational value, as well as skill, involved in co-operating together (see Chapter XIII). It may also serve as a preparation for the final vaulting by giving the feeling of the vault, such as when two people help a third "to get high", "Go upside down" or to "Fly". Having experienced the sensation with the assistance of her helpers a girl will know what to aim for when on her own, and will be more likely to achieve it.

The last part of the lesson is the **climax,** where the larger apparatus is used by small groups of girls. Here all the under-standing and ability gained earlier in the lesson is put into use. The apparatus provides a more difficult situation, a challenge or an obstacle involving height, width and often instability which has to be dealt with by the girls according to the task set, which in turn is dependent upon the theme of the lesson.

When the apparatus has been put away, the girls should work again on the floor for a very short time, to calm them down and bring them together as a whole class, before dismissal. It also ensures that the apparatus is put away carefully, that they all help each other and that the conscientious ones are not left to clear the gymnasium whilst the others dash for the showers.

2. *The theme of a lesson*

The teacher is helped, by having a lesson theme, to stress an aspect of movement. It is a movement guide which she can pursue, giving the experience to the class, guiding them to explore its possibilities and then developing it through the other aspects until as skilful a movement as possible is achieved. The theme is introduced in the first part of the lesson in a simple active way, then taught or deepened and developed on the floor, and finally in the climax used as a task on apparatus. All movement involves the use of the Body, Effort and the Space, but one must begin somewhere and the lesson theme establishes the starting point. It is possible to have more than one theme or movement stresses ; one aspect being the main theme and the second subsidiary, one of which should always be to do with the Body in order to give action in which to develop the other.

The choice of theme is affected by many factors such as age, ability, previous experience, the needs of the class and their interests. A gymnast starting with a first year class and continuing to teach them throughout the school could plan a syllabus of work to cover all aspects, some of which would be repeated, but taken to greater depth. If the gymnast is new in the school and therefore unaware of the work covered, she must observe the class closely in order to assess their movement needs, standard and ability. As a result of this she must then decide which themes to stress first and how to present them. She may find that a fourth or fifth year class need similar movement experiences to a first or second form, but due to their age and attitude towards gymnastics, she will have to present them differently.

There is no such thing as a typical class, but most **young seniors** (11-12 years) do tend to be agile, having light, pliable bodies with boundless energy, full of enthusiasm and eager to climb, jump and swing. The majority are unselfconscious, eager to prove themselves and enjoy having a goal or standard to aim for. They enjoy learning new things and often show great perseverance and determination to achieve.

In choosing suitable work for such a class these characteristics need to be exploited, therefore it is a time to give a good grounding in the fundamental aspects of movement. Transference of weight is being used continually, so this needs primary consideration in all its aspects, followed by the fundamental body actions with an awareness of the Weight Factor which causes the actions and developed through the use of the Time Factor and the Space until the girls have a good vocabulary.

Suitable themes are "Transference of Weight" (see Chapters II, III and IV) which includes all jumps, climbing and body manipulation ; "Bending and Stretching" (see Chapter V) ; "Twisting" (see Chapter VI) ; "Making parts of the Body Important" and "Parts meeting and parting" (see Chapter VII). These are a few suggestions and although all are main Body Themes, the teaching of the various tensions involved alongside the use of the body is essential. When the basic action is understood, variety and skill should be developed by the teacher guiding the class to explore the use of the Time Factor and the Space.

This age is quick to learn, enjoying repetition which leads to achievement. Their bodies are light and easy to manipulate therefore opportunity should be given to use all types of apparatus. As skill increases confidence grows and the girl has no fear, attacking the apparatus with vigour, the teacher secure in the fact that the girls are able to fall safely, having been taught soundly and given plenty of organised experience in saving themselves.

If classes have been well taught and the girls have gained

satisfaction through achievement, the interest will be maintained and the attitude of the **third and fourth** forms will be similar in many ways to that of the younger girls, but they may be more mature in that they appreciate an understanding of what is involved and why it is being done. They begin to take an interest in each other and so enjoy and benefit from helping each other by constructive criticism. They can also take more responsibility for each other when working in two's and three's.

The vocabulary of such girls should be good and they should be safe on apparatus : because of this, themes covered in the first and second years may be deepened and a higher standard of skill demanded, using more difficult apparatus or combined pieces. In addition Body Themes such as "Moving with Symmetry and Asymmetry" where the concentration is on the body relationship, whilst in the theme of "Moving in a balanced or an off-balanced way" the concentration is primarily on the adjustment of the body weight ; very soon, of course, both may become involved with each other. Then there are the more difficult Transference of Weight themes of "Being upside down" and "Flight" particularly. The selection of themes, with the use of suitable apparatus, should give the girls opportunity to put their skill into practice gaining real satisfaction. It is at this stage that many girls reach their climax in skill in gymnastics. Some grow rapidly, and to a certain degree lose their co-ordination or put on weight, which causes a temporary lack of ability and they may lose interest ; some never regain it, others do and will go on again and progress further.

The fourteen-fifteen age group tend to be rather more staid and sophisticated — both minds and bodies are maturing rapidly and soon become more self-conscious, often due to a feeling of inadequacy and insecurity leading to a lack of response and even unwillingness to work. This does not always happen, or may happen earlier, but if the class is known to the teacher she can more easily plan her work according to their needs and personalities. For the new teacher in a school this can be a difficult age group, for they tend not to trust a new person — it is a very conservative age. The first thing is to try to understand the girls as individuals, their changing moods, their lack of ability, their interests and ambitions. From the point of view of progression this stage is rather a plateau, and tasks should be set using familiar movement content, but presented differently. No new movement content should be introduced, for it is important for them to achieve and yet not to be made to feel that they are inferior and that they have done it all before. Much ingenuity and understanding on the part of the teacher is required at this stage, but it is an age when physical activity is of value to them.

As stated, fundamentally no new work should be tackled, but the skill involved in the themes already covered should be maintained. Some classes hate "Rolling" and "Taking weight on the hands", and so, as such, should be avoided for the time, but they usually enjoy and respond to working with a partner to fulfil a task, whether on the floor or on the apparatus, and this can make the familiar themes of renewed interest due to the additional relationships involved which are of great value (Chapter XIII). They are often interested in rhythm, therefore stress may be laid on the Effort themes whether in the nature of a Time or a Weight rhythm or the Flow as in "Going and Stopping". Space themes such as the use of Levels, Directions, Near and Far or Extensions are suitable. The apparatus (whether working alone, in two's or three's), should be of a suitable height, perhaps lower than one would hope, but combination and arrangement of pieces leads to interest.

If it is possible in the school, the **older girls** should be given some choice as to which aspects of Physical Education they pursue. Those who continue with gymnastics should be made aware of what they are doing, how and why, discussing with them the educational and physical values. They are intelligent individuals and need to be treated in an adult way; often they appreciate a truly intellectual approach to the work. They should be able to contribute considerably to the lessons, for they have greater understanding and interest and are able to take more responsibility.

The more advanced themes are suitable for this group, particularly those starting from some Space aspect such as "Central and Peripheral movement", the use of the "Planes of movement" and Effort themes. Apparatus may be combined or used more than once, and the girls themselves may be given opportunity to arrange their own apparatus, knowing the task. It may be that in a group there is a variety of ability though all are enthusiastic. This should be borne in mind when planning the apparatus and all abilities catered for — some will enjoy higher apparatus, whilst others fearing heights may use slightly lower apparatus, but the movement sequences they produce may require just as much skill though of a different nature.

All the above are only suggestions for themes of work, and every teacher should add to and adapt according to the girls in the school and make her own syllabus of work. The actual content and material of movement has been discussed in various chapters, but whatever is chosen as the theme of the lesson, it must involve the body and be supported by the other aspects of movement — *all are essential*. If a main BODY theme is used it must be developed through the Effort and Space. If a SPACE theme is used it must be developed through the use of the Body and Effort. If an EFFORT theme is used, through the use of the Body and Space.

3. *The development of a sequence*

The first thing is to **establish the movement experience** so that the class know what they are trying to do with their bodies and the tensions involved in order to achieve. The teacher needs to get the class moving with the minimum of explanation, teaching according to the age and ability of the class, being sure they understand, and giving time for them to practise.

Taking the theme of "Twisting" as an example, one way of introducing it to a class might be for the teacher to get the class to twist their hands one against the other, and then ask them to move their whole bodies in a similar way, the one end twisting against the other, until a transference of weight is caused.

Once they have experienced the action the next stage is **to explore** the possibilities in order to give variety and vocabulary. The teacher needs to **guide** the class to explore some of the many possibilities of movement; the range of variety varying according to the class. She may do this through the use of words, or demonstrations of ideas, as to the ways of using the Body (see chapters on the use of the Body), the Space (see chapters on Space), and the use of Effort (see chapters on Effort).

In the example of Twisting, transference of weight is involved throughout as the peak of each twist causes a transference of weight, during which an untwisting occurs in preparation for the next twisting action. This should result in a continuous rhythmic movement, the accent on the main twisting action and the recovery on the untwisting weight transference. Girls should therefore explore the possible parts of their bodies on which they can balance whilst twisting, which will affect which end of their bodies is free to initiate the twisting action. Space variations may be developed by guiding the class into the low, medium and high levels with a possible variation in the Extension in Space. The Weight Factor will have been used to achieve the original twisting action, but now it should be deepened to give accent and rhythm to the movement by increasing the tension involved in the twisting and therefore a greater reduction of tension in the recovery. The twisting may be done quickly or slowly so combining the Elements of Firmness with Suddenness or Sustainment and the Fine Touch recovery with the opposite

Element of the Time Factor ; thus there may be variation in the use of the Time Factor. The combination of the two Factors with that of Flow leads to resilience. If the Flow Factor is Bound, the movement is withheld and over-careful, whereas with the freedom of Flow the Time and Weight Factors interplay and the movement bounces, is elastic and resilient.

By now the class will have experienced many ways of moving and amassed a certain vocabulary of ideas and the time has come to **form a sequence,** which means selecting from the many ways and using them logically to form a series of movement phrases (a sequence). A method often used by inexperienced teachers, and unfortunately *not* a very success-ful one, is "choose three ideas and put them together". It often happens that three such ideas chosen at random *do not* follow logically one to the next, which is so essential for flow and ease of movement. Perhaps a better way is for the teacher to get her class to establish a starting position and guide the length of sequence.

In the case of Twisting the starting position could be on any of the parts of the body they have found suitable — then for the girls to move freely for a short time when the teacher stops them and they hold their final position. She can then ask the class to repeat exactly what they have just done. Thus she guides the length of sequence and out of the freedom of moving the sequence should be logical.

With older, more experienced girls it may be sufficient to ask for "A sequence using Twisting". Here the length of sequence is left to the girls and now becomes part of the task, their judgement having to be used.

After this initial stage of making the sequence the girls need to consider what they did in the sequence, and with the help of the teacher, perhaps reject and re-select from their vocab-ulary. When all are satisfied that there is variety in the use of the Body, the use of Space and the Effort content and that the phrases follow logically, the girls need to work on that *same* sequence until it is as skilled as is possible for that individual to achieve.

Skill of performance is the result of repetition of movement with a deepening of the content of the action. It is at this stage particularly that the teacher is able to give individual help. If taught well the whole class will understand what is involved and with practice will achieve a standard, but individuals find different aspects difficult ; one girl may need help with some moment of weight transference, another with the use of direction, whilst another the rhythm of the Effort content.

The girls should work on their sequence for several lessons, gradually improving the skill of movement, being self-critical and selecting particular aspects to work on until the whole performance is enriched and skilful. In building and working on such a sequence the movement memory and vocabulary are increased, the logical flow of movement improved, the powers of selection and judgement encouraged, and the repetition with deepening of content gives skill and understanding of movement, leading to confidence and satisfaction.

The girls will have experienced the movement on the floor and will now be able to use it in conjunction with the apparatus, the teacher selecting a suitable task in conjunction with her choice of apparatus. For example, "Get off with a Twist" or "Twist as you go along". The progress on the apparatus is similar to that on the floor — experiencing the movement, exploring the possibilities on that apparatus, then selecting and forming a sequence (vault) which is worked on until skilfully accomplished.

4. *Classes whose previous training has been of a more formal nature*

These girls will have been told exactly what to do and when to move, therefore they will be at a complete loss if asked to explore the possibilities of a task or to make their own sequences. They may not understand what is involved or have any ideas, nor may they have the confidence to work on their own, being used to a class rhythm with a unison response.

Since it is the girls in the class who are our main concern whatever their previous experience of movement, the teacher must start from where they are in movement. With such a class the teacher may have to make up and teach, by demonstration, a definite movement sequence suitable to their ability and vocabulary. This in itself will most likely be different from their previous work, where repetition of the same action may have taken place, the flow of movement with its variety in weight transference, Time-Weight rhythms, use of Levels and Directions will make it very different, so it must be fairly simple at first.

After the demonstration the teacher may have to guide the class with her voice, but gradually she should try to get them to work on their own. The actions used in the above sequence might then be used in a slightly different order, each girl choosing for herself. This would necessitate a certain amount of individual work, but they have the security of being aware of the content. A rhythm might be given, the whole class responding to it, but making their own sequence. This is particularly useful with the use of the legs in the Introductory part of the lesson ; starting from known actions such as stepping and jumping — the rhythm given should set the Effort content which the teacher must make the girls aware of, and then guide them into simple variations of weight transference using the feet and the more obvious directions.

The essential thing is to maintain their confidence, but to enlarge and widen their conception of movement with understanding, making them more self-reliant and independent.

5. *Presentation of the work and contact with classes*

In presenting work to classes the teacher should try to get them moving with as little explanation as possible, starting from something which they can do, and then through observation or by placing particular stress on the aspect she wishes them to experience. They will need encouragement, whether it be generally to the whole class or to individuals, for a task has been set and they may need urging to persevere, the teacher gradually helping them to achieve. Their minds need to be on the task knowing what is involved at the moment and anticipating what is to happen next. Skill is only achieved through much repetition of movement and the deepening of the content and the teacher must allow time to achieve it. She should always aim for a standard slightly greater than is voluntarily given, maintaining movement which has already been taught. In this way the standard and vocabulary will grow with each new aspect taught. She should progress her work at the rate of the majority of the class, but be aware of and provide for the variety in ability, giving help to the less able as well as the more able girls. It is the effort made and the progress as an individual that is of importance.

The teacher may present her work in a variety of ways; she may explain, use contrast of movement, demonstrate either herself or select one of the girls. When using a girl to demonstrate it is better to select a "good" one, and if there is need to contrast it with a "bad" one the teacher herself can show that. During a period of exploration it is often wise to warn the girl selected that she is to show her idea, so that she knows what to do and can therefore demonstrate with confidence. In all demonstrations the teacher should state clearly what the class is to observe, whether it be quite definite or in the nature of a definite question. If she fails to do this, since there is so much to observe, she may get many true observations, but *not* the one she wishes for at the moment. It is also very much easier to observe one girl than if two or three move at the same time.

It is essential that the lesson is thoroughly prepared; that the teacher knows what experience she wishes the girls to have, why she is teaching it, what is involved, and how to present it to the class. She needs to have an enthusiasm for her work which in turn influences her classes.

Contact with the girls is essential to gain their confidence and to inspire them to wish to learn ; the more they desire to achieve the better will be the results and the greater the enjoyment and satisfaction, provided the teacher gives opportunity and a steady progression of work. She must make herself clear to the class using everyday words, being able to explain her wishes in more ways than one, and making full use of the intelligence of the girls.

She should present her work enthusiastically, if it is of no value she should not be teaching it. She must remember that the experience is new to the class and therefore exciting — she has experienced the situation many times and it is easy to forget the first thrill she had many years ago — so she needs to enter into the spirit of the lesson and re-live it again with her class.

She must be ready to praise and encourage effort made, if the result is skilful all the better, but it is the learning and all that goes into it that matters most. The teacher needs to be alive and active in mind and body, moving among the class being aware of every girl, so letting them realise that every girl is of importance and that she is willing to help every one of them, whether she is near to them or in the far corner of the gymnasium. She should speak so that all can hear her, so that what she says to one girl, another girl can apply to her own movement.

There are many opportunities when the class can contribute to the lesson, remembering that movement questions should be answered in movement, rather than by words, and this should be encouraged so that the girls feel it is their lesson in co-operation with the teacher.

The teacher should try to get to know the girls as individuals, their difficulties, hopes, fears, triumphs and successes as well as their movement, which is often indicative of their personalities.

Gymnastics is a medium through which the teacher hopes to help towards the education of the girls and to prepare them for life. She should try to be a source of stability and guidance, always there ready and willing to help, showing patience and understanding, always trying to inculcate high standards, sound judgements and independence in her pupils.

CHAPTER XV

Observation

OBSERVATION is most essential in teaching today, for it is as a result of this that the teacher knows what to coach, summing up the ability of the girls and planning the work as a result. There is no set progression of exercises and agilities as there was at one time, when a list could be consulted. This may have been of some use, from the untrained teacher's point of view, for it did enable her to progress steadily through the numerical list, but it was of little value to the girls, for all do not progress at the same rate, nor do they need the same help, and at its best it could be only a setting of certain situations and not truly teaching the girls according to their needs.

In education today we are trying to deal with individual human beings with their many differences. Before, only the average was considered. We now realise this was wrong in movement, as one person may be excellent in one aspect but poor in another. We therefore aim to assess through observation what the class as a whole needs, and then within the task, set out to help the individual at whatever stage or with whatever aspect of movement she most needs. As observation is essential to the teacher when teaching, it is also an aid to the girls when learning, imitation being the most instinctive method.

At this point it might be wise to consider what is involved when observing. Every action is preceded by and maintained through **mental action.** This is of utmost importance, for without the right preparation the resulting action will not be satisfactory. In the first instance the **attention** of the performer has to be gained and so focussed on the task in hand.

She then needs to have a certain **intention** or desire to fulfil the task, followed by a **decision** which sets the action into motion, which should continue with **precision** until completed. These stages of mental preparation thus involve the attention, intention and decision of a person before the physical action even starts. As physical action involves Effort so does mental action, the initial or **attention** stage having a connection with the Space Factor, being either Direct or Flexible. In gymnastics the task is known and the girls should set their minds directly on the task. A flexible attention might lead a teacher to such a remark as "Think what you are to do — concentrate." The second stage of **intention** is linked with the Weight Factor and to achieve anything it is necessary to have a Firm desire to fulfil the task. A Weak intention would be that of a girl who was not trying to achieve. The third stage of **decision** is linked with the Time Factor being either Sudden or Sustained, if too sudden the decision may be hasty or if too sustained the action never starts, different problems will need different attitudes towards the Time Factor, but excess in either direction may lead to disaster. The Factor of Flow is connected with the fulfilment of the action or **precision** whether withheld and careful as with Bound Flow or more resilient and flowing with Free Flow, depending on the movement necessary. Observation of these stages of the mental attitude of the girls are often ignored and all or one of them may be the cause of poor movement or even accidents.

Observation of the **physical action**, strictly speaking, is confined to looking, using the sense of sight, but if the kinesthetic sense or feeling of the muscle action involved is experienced together with the hearing of explanations, three senses of the body are brought into action. It stands to reason that if three senses are used instead of one, the results should be better ; in practice this is also true. In experimenting it will be found that if person A, using only her eyes, watches person B move, and then A tries to copy her, a certain likeness is achieved : but if A moves with B and so gets a kinesthetic impression as well, the result is nearer the original : the most accurate result is achieved if B helps A in addition by saying what, how and where she is moving — here there is a combination of the three senses of seeing, kinesthetic feeling and hearing. Therefore when observing movement as many of the senses as possible should be brought into action. The teacher can use her eyes and also feel the action within her own body.

When the girls observe under the direction of the teacher, she is able to explain before or whilst the demonstration is taking place, thus the girls can hear as well as use their eyes, and can feel it within themselves as they watch ; attention having been drawn to the mental preparation of the demonstrator as well as the physical performance.

Each class should have a scheme of work made by the teacher as a result of her observation of the class as a whole ; this helps her to maintain a standard of teaching and to plan an all-round experience of movement for each class. To do this she must judge the standard of work the class has achieved, noting aspects which need most help and therefore the work to be covered. With this, the ability and rate of learning needs to be assessed so that she does not progress either too slowly or too quickly — it is bad to do either, for both lead to dissatisfaction on the part of the class.

At whatever stage the class is at, there is usually exploration of the task, followed by working for skill of movement. Whichever it is, the teacher needs to observe what the body is doing, how and where it is moving. At the exploratory stage she can make suggestions as to the use of the Body, Effort or Space which will lead the girls to increase their movement vocabulary. Similarly in the achievement of a skilled action, the whole sequence needs watching and a decision made as to what aspect will help the class as a whole, or the individual, to improve. Besides observing the content of the movement the teacher should see that the sequence has purpose, one movement leading logically to the next. Girls often need help in selecting from the many ideas they have discovered whilst exploring, some of which may not be profitable, nor follow on logically one to another — all help given depends upon observation by the teacher.

The teacher needs to observe well in order to select from among the class one girl who can demonstrate for the rest of the class to watch, whether it be to show an idea or the skill in doing. She needs to choose the best possible, and this in all probability will not, and should not always be, the same girl, pointing out to them the mental preparation as well as the physical manipulation of the body and getting them to experience the movement inside themselves as they watch.

Besides the teacher herself observing her class, she should help the girls in the observation of each other ; watching other girls' ideas in movement helps to widen vocabulary and leads to the discovery of further ideas. It enables girls to see an action done skilfully and sets a standard to aim for, which encourages greater effort. It leads to a greater understanding of what good movement is and what it entails, making for clarity, precision and selection. To see other girls demonstrate gives confidence to the more timid to pursue and with practice achieve, knowing it is possible, and that they have the right idea.

If girls can observe they are able to help each other, criticising positively, so they learn to give and take criticism in the right way. Through seeing many people moving success- fully, but in different ways, the girls begin to recognise that there are different ways of achieving, most of which are successful ; if they are not they become able to make helpful suggestions. They learn tolerance and an awareness that one cannot be good at everything ; they recognise one individual's ability in ideas, another's in certain aspects of skill in move- ment. They become more aware and observant of what is happening around them, whether from a safety point of view, as concerning apparatus, or in helping each other. All this helps them to take responsibility and to be aware of what is going on around which one hopes they will automatically use outside the gymnasium.

Observation of the class in general is of value to the teacher in getting to know and understand the girls, how to treat them, to get the best from them, and to help them to maturity. Help may be given in setting of standards in the appearance and habits of the class : the clothes they wear and how they care for them, the regular use of showers, the opening of windows, swabbing of the floor to make it suitable to roll on and work with bare feet. The teacher should be conscious of any girl who seems off-colour or injured, in fact the well-being of the individual should be her concern.

It is also of value to observe the mood of the class. If it is their normal mood, whether it be over-excitable or lethargic, the teacher can be prepared for it and plan her work accordingly, but a normally enthusiastic class may, on occasion, be very depressed and the teacher must try to change this through suitable movement. If unobservant she would go on unaware, teach the girls nothing and fail to help them mentally. As the teacher gets to know the class she should also become aware of individual temperaments of the girls, those who are afraid in certain situations ; the ones with few ideas who need to be given extra confidence and encouragement ; the bossy girl who needs help in order to accept a leader ; and the timid one who needs urging to take the lead ; the girl who responds to a challenge and the one who needs persuasion — the girls need knowing as people as well as in movement, though the one is often indicative of the other. What are their movement habits ? Have they a favourite movement pattern which they repeat continually and often quite skilfully ? The teacher should observe and try to remember, so that she can guide them to explore further and so widen their movement vocabulary, whether through the use of the Body, the Effort, or the Space.

When teaching the teacher needs to observe whether the class is working to capacity and their attitude towards the work and to teach them accordingly. She should continually be asking herself such questions as "Do they understand ?", "Are they gaining the experience planned ?", "Do they need more practice in order to gain satisfaction ?", "Have they felt a peak of achievement and is it time to change the activity ?" All this has to be noted irrespective of the standard of movement, for that will depend on the age, ability and past training of the class.

The teacher must be continually alert and observant in order to prevent accidents, although she should train the girls themselves to take this responsibility, it is finally hers, in such things as seeing that the floor is clear with nothing to trip over ; that it has not been recently polished and is slippery ; that the apparatus is lifted and carried sensibly and placed in suitable places and that it is secure.

Some of the points made in this chapter will be dealt with at once as an immediate result of observation. Others, once having been seen, can be considered for the next lesson, but whichever it might be, the value of acute observation cannot be too highly stressed — it is vitally essential to the teacher and of value to the girls.

CHAPTER XVI

Poise

GOOD poise is indicative of the whole attitude of a person involving both mental and bodily poise ; the two sides cannot be separated, the one influencing the other ; thus lack of poise or poor posture may have either a mental or physical origin.

A person who is poised might be described as having confidence, showing a certain independence and dignity, who has an easy upright carriage, being easily balanced and moving with a flow of movement. Ideally a **sound movement training should achieve this,** but if a girl adopts and forms bad habits, whether due to current fashions, rapid growth or an intense stage of shyness, she may need special help to combat the effect. The Educational gymnast has no control over some of the causes of poor posture, such as very late nights causing fatigue and leading to slack carriage, the wearing of unsuitable shoes when away from school so affecting the feet, and she can only advise ; but she can help by setting a good example herself and by planning sound movement lessons which give the girls a sense of poise both mentally and physically, with an understanding of what is involved in carrying oneself well.

It sometimes happens that several girls in one class have a certain physical weakness such as a poking head and round shoulders, and if nothing is done about it a permanent habit may be formed. In such a case, the gymnast, having observed the need of her class, can give special consideration to it and plan her work accordingly. A normal Educational lesson will be taken but with particular stress put on that particular area of the body which needs the special attention, selecting tasks which give opportunity to make the girls more aware of the correct use and relationship of that part of the body to the rest — thus it may be possible to prevent bad habits becoming permanent which later may lead to real deformity.

The most common postural weaknesses are weak or flat feet, knock-knees, poking head and round shoulders (kyphosis), a forward tilt of the pelvis causing a hollow back (Lordosis), uneven shoulders or hips with some twisting of the spine (scoliosis) and a giving way to weight resulting in general slackness. In all these cases the girls need to become aware of the particular area of the body, what the fault is and why it should be corrected, so that there is *real co-operation* with the teacher, who should help through her choice of work to strengthen the weakened muscles, break down the bad habit and re-educate the correct use and relationships of the parts of the body concerned.

Weak or Flat Feet may be recognised by a flattened arch of the foot with the weight of the body falling onto the inner, instead of the outer border of the feet. This is often the result of wearing shoes which are too small or narrow with too high a heel, not allowing normal use of the feet with correct carriage of the body weight. Girls with such feet need advice on their footwear and in their lessons to be taught how to use their feet correctly.

A lesson with a stress on the feet should ensure full use of them throughout, so strengthening the muscles and making the girls aware of their correct use. Perhaps the first essential is to make the class conscious of the parts of the feet and their correct use when walking. The body weight should be directly over the back foot, each part of the foot being used in turn to propel the body forward and should be sufficient to move the body weight forwards consecutively onto the heel, outside border, ball of the foot, and toes of the front foot, which should now be completely supporting the body weight : with the continuity of this action the body weight is carried smoothly and directly from one foot to the other. Incorrect adjustment of the body weight, which may be carried too far back or too far forwards, results in compensation in the hip joints and spine, in order to maintain balance. This everyday action of walking, where the right foot is used, followed by the left, is more complicated than at first thought, for to walk well each part of the foot has to be used in turn, both in the receiving leg and the pushing off leg with correct adjustment of the body weight. It is often overlooked. To train efficient use of the feet they need to be bare in movement lessons or in soft pliable shoes, which merely act as a protection from a poor floor surface, allowing free use of all joints of the feet.

Besides the teaching of correct walking, the right way of using the feet is of importance in all stepping, running and jumping, all of which help to strengthen muscles if used correctly. In using apparatus various balances, travelling up inclined forms to poise on the feet, steppings involving different heights and widths, use the feet and require adjustment of the body weight over them. Stronger muscle work will be involved in climbing activities using hands and feet to grip the apparatus ; all jumping activities onto and off apparatus where particular stress can be put on the "take off" and the "landing" where the feet should be used correctly. The height of the apparatus should be increased gradually as the strength and use of the feet increases. The use of high apparatus will defeat its own ends if used before the feet are strong enough to carry the weight correctly of the falling body.

The feet are in constant use carrying the body weight about and it is essential that they should be used correctly. If they are, they should be strong and cause no pain, if not, each step taken incorrectly puts a strain on already weak muscles and will exaggerate the fault and in time cause pain.

Knock-knees are often associated with flat feet, the one may be the cause or the result of the other, so besides trying to help the knock-knees note should be taken of the feet also. Knock-knees may be recognised by the knocking or overlapping of the knees when standing with the feet together, often causing a bending of one or both knees : again the body weight falls onto the insides of the feet and the legs turn or rotate inwards. In such cases the weakened muscles are those which stretch the knee (Extensors) and those which turn the leg outwards and lift the one leg sideways away from the other (Abductors). These muscles need strengthening by the choice of suitable tasks and the correct use and relationship of the legs and the feet needs teaching.

Correct use of the feet needs teaching as for flat feet but with special awareness of the relationship of the knees to the feet. The knees should fall directly forward over the feet. Such actions as stepping, but especially in a sideways direction, which should involve abduction and outward rotation ; leg gestures in similar directions and simple jumps and landings on the feet are valuable. In fact all leg parting, circling outwards and extension, whether the body weight is taken on the legs or on other parts of the body, are of use in strengthening the weaker muscles. Any of these may be used in conjunction with the apparatus such as stepping sideways, leg circling outwards leading to turning on bars, leg parting on the window-ladder or horse. Landing on the feet is again of importance and should be progressed as with weak feet, but since there is a weakness in the knee joint with knock-knees, landing after a turning jump should at first be avoided as this puts particular strain onto the knee joint.

A **Poking Head** often accompanies **Round Shoulders** (Kyphosis) and may be the result of rapid growth, the girl being unable to control this increased height. Muscles of the upper back need strengthening and an awareness of the relationship of the head and upper spine needs establishing especially when sitting and standing. It is the duty of *every* teacher, but especially of the gymnast, to help these girls to understand how to sit and stand correctly.

Some girls grow and develop more rapidly than their contemporaries and are sometimes self-conscious about this and tend to stoop in order to hide the fact : in such cases the cause is really psychological and should be dealt with by an understanding teacher alongside the necessary physical help.

Good carriage of the head and spine is important, for if the upper spine is out of alignment the lower spine will compensate, in order to maintain balance, and a secondary postural fault may appear ; the lungs become cramped and work less efficiently combined with the general lack of poise and confidence.

Lessons may be prepared with a stress on the awareness of the upper spine. These should include work for the weakened upper spine extensors and the transverse shoulder muscles combined with an awareness of the relationship of the head and upper spine. Activities involving a rising or spreading action such as "Stepping onto a form and poise" gives time to sense the correct relationship. All varieties of Bending and Stretching with a stress on the *stretching* give excellent opportunity to use the muscles and to train alignment of the head and spine, particularly if other planes of movement are used, thus establishing a true kinesthetic sense of the relationship.

When apparatus is used there is opportunity for much stronger muscle work, and care is needed so as not to increase the fault ; should this happen it is an indication that the task set is too difficult at this stage. All types of hanging and swinging using bars and ropes involve very strong use of the vertical and transverse muscles of the back, as the whole weight of the body is carried on the arms. Slightly easier muscle work is involved in climbing activities where the body weight is shared between the arms and the legs. Other apparatus may be used such as a horse, box or springboard, where a stretch is involved, or poising on or walking along apparatus. When planning apparatus work, care should be taken to include tasks involving varying degrees of strength of muscle work and opportunity for slower and quicker adjustment of the head and spine relationship, for the faster the action the less time there is to achieve the correct alignment.

Hollow Back or Lordosis is an increase forward of the normal curve in the lower spine with a tilting forward of the pelvis. The increased curve forward of the lower spine causes a hollow back and a protruding abdomen, the Abdominal and Gluteal (seat) muscles becoming overstretched thus allowing the pelvis to tilt forwards, so that the organs in the pelvis are less well supported and may give trouble in later life. In such a situation these two big muscle groups need strengthening in order to maintain the correct tilt of the pelvis, and restore correct alignment of the lower spine and pelvis.

Activities involving extension of the hip joint such as gestures, steps, leg swingings (particularly backwards) and jumping help to strengthen the Gluteal muscles. Twisting and curling of the spine, particularly if taken to the limit of movement, makes use of the abdominal muscles. Pelvic tilting is essential to co-ordinate both the muscle groups where the front of the pelvis is pulled upwards by the Abdominal muscles and the back of the pelvis is pulled downwards by the Gluteal muscles.

Apparatus may be used to encourage the use of and so the strengthening of the Abdominal muscles in any task which involves bringing the knees high towards the shoulders as in curled inverted hanging on ropes or bars, getting onto high apparatus with the feet or rolling. Tasks involving straightening of the hip joint such as jumping off apparatus such as forms or boxes use the Gluteal muscles. Help throughout the lesson should be given with the correction of the pelvic tilt in relation to the whole of the spine and included in a similar way as with Kyphosis, but now the attention will be laid primarily on the lower spine.

In **Scoliosis** there is lateral curvature of the spine whilst the vertebrae rotate to the opposite side. This is recognised by uneven hip and or shoulder levels with some turning — for example the left shoulder may be lower than the right with the head and shoulders turning slightly to the right.

Most people have a slight form of this fault due to such things as standing temporarily on one leg (affecting the lower spine), carrying cases or bags under the same arm (affecting the upper spine), or sitting always crossing the same leg, but if the habit is started and established in youth and allowed to continue, permanent harm may be caused and pain result. The fault is therefore caused by the uneven use of the muscles on either side of the spine, so it is the task of the gymnast to see that these muscles are used equally. Equal stress is therefore necessary on both sides of the body and if there is a difference in height of either shoulder or hip, re-education in symmetrical carriage is necessary. Many people have a favourite side and if left completely free, use only that side, whether it be a leg to jump from or a way of twisting and turning the body. Thus if an asymmetric task is set, *both* sides should be stressed in turn. This, of course, should be considered at all times in *every* lesson and not only after the weakness has appeared, but if it has, particular stress should be laid on using the less favourite side whatever the theme of the lesson.

All the above start with a weakness of certain muscle groups, which if allowed to persist result in the bones and joints being affected, but the last postural fault is due to a flabbiness, or **lack of tension in all the muscles** of the body which gives rise to a slouching, lethargic action and a general giving way.

This may be due to an attitude of mind, as the mind affects a person's movement, and so must be taken into consideration, but movement also has an effect on a person's mind and so the problem may be helped by movement. In such a case it is essential that the lesson should be particularly stimulating and challenging, both mentally and physically, to gain the interest and co-operation of the class. It is the tension in the muscles that is lacking and this links very much with grit and determination and a positive attitude towards life : the work therefore needs to be challenging and of a dynamic nature, with a stress on the Weight and Time Factors of movement leading to body precision. Stress should be put on the interplay of weak and strong tensions in various ways with the crescendos and diminuendos in such activities as "Run and jump", whether on the floor or using apparatus with some means of the individual measuring her own achievement. "Co-operating with a partner to get high" involves a build up of tension both in the one going high and the one who is helping, and the feeling of power in the muscles should be encouraged in order to achieve such a task.

In work on the apparatus the Weight rhythm should again be stressed, the moment of strong tension as against weaker tension, whether in a single vault or a repetitive sequence where the apparatus is used more than once. Simple apparatus such as a form, low bar, or a series of little boxes as well as the higher apparatus can be used most successfully, the girls repeating their movement phrase several times with resilience as they use the length of the apparatus which leads to a repetitive rhythm. The "take off" and "recovery" from any vault are important — it is often most noticeable at these moments that these girls fail, not achieving the strong sudden impact of the "take off" nor the resilient "recovery" on meeting the floor, so often just flopping off the apparatus. These girls need encouraging to attack and make an effort, until through some measure of success there is a desire to achieve, which in turn leads to greater success and satisfaction. This state is the opposite to the giving way, hanging back attitude of the lethargic and uninterested.

During the one or two periods per week of Educational Gymnastics the gymnast should set out, as part of her normal lesson, to help the girls to understand *why* they should carry themselves well, and teach them *how* to do so, giving them the kinesthetic awareness of good poise alongside the balanced movement education.

In normal circumstances, if taught well, none of the above postural faults should arise; however, if there is a class with a tendency towards a weakness, it should be dealt with at once, the teacher guiding the individuals into knowing what is correct, and then it is the continual hour by hour, day by day persistence on the part of the individual that matters until a new and good habit is formed.

Index